Edward A. Dougherty

SELECTED POEMS

FUTURECYCLE PRESS
www.futurecycle.org

Cover image, fox portrait by AZemdega; author photo by Beth Bentley; cover and interior design by Diane Kistner; Gentium Book Basic text and Cronos Pro titling

NOTE
Except for stylistic differences, the poems appear
as published in the represented collections.

Library of Congress Control Number: 2025937642

Published by FutureCycle Press
Athens, Georgia, USA

ISBN 978-1-952593-52-9

This book is for Beth,
my dearest companion
in this luminous house.

Even the earth on which I walked was luminous.

—Marc Chagall

Contents

Foreword...8

from
PILGRIMAGE TO A GINGKO TREE

Guest..12
Pilgrimage to a Gingko Tree...13
Crossing Motoyasu Bridge...14
Delta...15
Gingko..17
Tancho (Cranes)..18

from
THE METAL OF MY MOUTH

Why I Think About Hiroshima & Nagasaki....................20
The Missing...21
Times Like These..22
Passing-bell...23
Like Superman..24
Something about Peace..25

from
THE LUMINOUS HOUSE

Coming to Bloom..28
Ancient Sound (I)...29
Dance of the Mournful Child..30
Mr. Z...31
Mr. Z...32
Full Moon..33
Love Song by the New Moon..35
Ancient Sound (II)...36
This Star Teaches Bending..37
The Forgetful Angel...38
Mr. Z...39
The Light and So Much Else...40

from
PILGRIMAGE TO A GINGKO TREE

Another Journey...42
In the Shadow of Shirakiyama...43
Origami...44
Cosmos...45
Aioi...46

All Burning...47
The Night Cafe..48
Harvest Moon-viewing...49
The Bridge..50
At the Calligraphy Festival...51
Passing...52
Sandankyo...53
The Sower...54

from
PART DARKNESS, PART BREATH

Into Darkness..56
The Maple Leaf Elegy..58
Fishing Boats on the Beach...59
First Frost..60
Bedrock...61
Walking Meditation...62
Story..66
Almost...68
Fossil...69
Passing Steve's Field...70
Holder Of My Dreams...72
How Ants Felled Two Trees...73
Nothing To Do With Decoration...74
Grace Street..75

from
EVERYDAY OBJECTS

The Romantic Quest..78
The Bathtub...79
Everyday Shames: Parenthood...80
you do the math..81
Stuart Little, Yellow House, Avalon, NJ....................................82
Thanksgiving...83
Everyday Shames: Scouting...84
(With Roethke) In a Watery Drowse..86
R5: The Paoli Local...90
The Display Models...91
The Discontent of Everyday Objects..92
To One Born in a Time of Crisis..94
The History of Love...96
More Light...98
Moonlight on Snow..99

Humility...100
Another Secret Letter (to my mother)..101
Everyday Shames: Pee-wee Football..102
A Favorite Memory Echoed in a Line from a Favorite Poem............104
A Blessing...105
Twins..106
Emptiness (The Middle Way)..107
The Vow...108
Voluptuous..109
In a Cedar Tub...110

from
HOUSE OF GREEN WATER

Gorge..112
Self-Portrait, In the Eye of Stone..113
Spring Pond Song..114
At the Shelter..115
At the Fire Station...116
From Source to Mouth..118
Seneca...120

from
BACKYARD PASSAGES and GRACE STREET

White on White..122
Drought-Dry Heart..124
Chicory Flower Song..127
Backyard Passage..129
Snow-Country Sojourn..132
The Green Spiral..136

from
10048

Blowback...142
from Gambits...143
Displacement...145
from Descent...147
from Imagination, And Its Limits..149
Sound Waves...151
The Tallest Building in the World...154
from Corrugated..156
from Gravity..159
from Domino Theory..161
Freefall..162
Diligence...165

from Echoes...168
The Afghan Trap...169
Project Safe Flight...172
Preserving the Fabric..174

Notes...176
Acknowledgments..178

Foreword

Many years ago, in a small town in upstate New York, Edward invited me to join a group of poets who met at his home each Wednesday night. We would read aloud and help one another with our writing. Summers, we'd sometimes circle around his backyard firepit, glimpse deer interested in his wife's lush vegetable garden, and read into the darkness until, eyes straining, we'd relocate inside. I remember an Audubon clock in the living room that featured different birds chiming away. Ten o'clock, our witching hour, I believe, might have been warbled by a bluebird. We were all different birds, too, with diverse styles, backgrounds and poetic voices. Here, years ago, I first heard many of these poems in their crystalline stage.

In addition to the task at hand, we'd veer off topic, as right-brained poets often do. Edward's an impassioned storyteller and shared many anecdotes: tales of growing up outside of Philly; his being a "weirdly spiritual kid" glorying in early morning Mass in his altar boy robes; the chaos of dinner tables with his seven siblings; his dad, who worked for IBM, commuting into the city, returning each day as if from Mount Olympus. Often we'd all rake through political news of the day, bemoaning next invasions, continued injustices. Always there were stories about undergrad creative writing students he worked with. Not all great poets are great teachers, but Edward's the real deal. These stories would be followed by "What are you reading?" Poetry books would magically appear from backroom shelves. At the front of each volume, he would have meticulously listed page numbers, quotes, tiny inked post-it-note love notes to *his* teachers.

The genesis of this book formally began with writing at Penn State, where Edward majored in Creative Writing and minored in Religious Studies. After receiving his MFA at Bowling Green, he and Beth volunteered for two and a half years serving as hosts at the World Friendship Center at Hiroshima. Half of the members of the board of this organization were survivors of the atomic bomb. Many of the visitors to this center had their own stories or had travelled there to have questions answered. Some he could answer; others were more difficult. How do you answer the seemingly unanswerable questions? Begin with words. Follow them. Work relentlessly.

The poems collected here span a lifetime and are arranged chronologically. Images in "Ancient Sound" set the stage for what will follow: "below the crash of circumstance/ the faithful hum/ the constant song/ the earth sounds through/ and death/ has no place in it/ step down and tune yourself." A poet, before turning to the world, must first tune himself. This wordsmithing is an inward spiritual journey, accomplished through meditation, silence, deep reading and heightened listening. Here writing and devotion intertwine ("I live at a spirit address"). This is not an ivory-tower, esoteric enterprise. The world clambers on with its catastrophes and horrors; examining the lives of those in distress becomes a moral obligation, a calling. This radical empathy and hospitality extends in all directions and crosses geographical and temporal boundaries.

Where will these poems take you? At times, the speaker merges with the landscape, becomes transcendentalist, entering trees or plants, or likens himself to a canyon carved by ancient waters. The landscapes are rural and urban, interior and exterior, local and exotic, real and mythic. Nothing is too small ("clothespins...enjoying the wooden/ click of congregating") or too flawed to be worthy of attention ("on the compass-face, more cardinal points/ than *victim* and *executioner*"). This poet becomes the host ("the welcome mat collects/ the detritus of the world"). As self empties out, space appears. The poet ("I, whatever/ that upright pronoun means") steps into the world, then steps aside to better enter into it. From this absence, a presence.

When Edward first shared some of his poems about 9/11 with our group, I remember him saying, "How could I not write about this?" Looking at the worldwide cataclysms of both Hiroshima and 9/11 means confronting some of the ways in which we are truly terrible. How do you enter these horrors? "I am a bell/ the metal of my mouth rings." While traveling cross-country, Beth "reads aloud...she does all the voices." Edward does this too. Empathy makes of him a master ventriloquist. He speaks all the voices: the bedrock, the generals, the 40,000 doors, jihadists, workers, the victims. It's an operatic feat, this orchestra of language vivifying and transforming what was lost.

Conversely, often the language is a solo instrument, clear, chiseled, and spare. These poems are elegant constructions fashioned from ordinary words. At times, you may hear echoes of Bashō or Issa ("Willows listen,/ their fine tips descending./ Uncurling like seahorses"). Images comes to life with lyric simplicity and musicality (a simple night with his sister Julie, "listening to their mother's voice/ over the constant rush of rain"). Narrative poems appear side by side with odes, where a bathtub turns philosophical ("to be empty, to open/ itself to the limitless/ out of which all things/ emerge and back into which/ they sink") and a lovesick extension cord "quietly crackles." Gorgeous language ("Yellow flowers on tall stalks/ stand like lanterns/ above thinning rice fields") calls to mind Hiroshige's landscapes. In the later poems gathered here, the poet experiments with line and form, bending time and sprawling into a harmonic mix of reportage, political memos, oral history, architectural blueprints, editorials, first person narratives, and interior monologues.

In the poem "In a Watery Drowse," the speaker quotes Theodore Roethke and confesses, "Thoughts I thought were new/ turn up tendrilled and rooted/ in yours." Poets often echo the styles of those who first cracked their hearts open. In his book *Journey Work: Crafting a Life of Poetry and Spirit*, Edward examines his own poetic path and claims many mentors. Denise Levertov tutored him "in her fusing of moment-by-moment attentiveness with social conscience." Carolyn Forché modeled the poet as witness and defender of the weak. Galway Kinnell's longer meditations that meld the spiritual with the natural became beacons. In addition to writers, visual artists serve as catalysts. Calligraphers teach simplicity. Van Gogh's fishing boats sail into Biblical waters where doubt and belief are tested.

In *A History of Reading,* Alberto Manguel claims, "We read in slow, long motions, as if drifting in space, weightless.... And sometimes, when the stars are kind, we read with an intake of breath, with a shudder...as if a memory had suddenly been rescued from a place deep within us—the recognition of something we never knew was there...."

Edward A. Dougherty, much like his mythical creation Mr. Z, is a star carrier, a poet of great skill, depth, and humanity. His poems make the earth more luminous.

—Margaret Kasper Reed
Author of *Lament's Grocery, Poetry of Elmira*

from
PILGRIMAGE TO A GINGKO TREE

(World Friendship Center, 1995)

Guest

after Morishita-sensei's calligraphy

To welcome the wind,
singing and lonely, the pine trees
make themselves
a suitable home, the way
a man will write his name
in the shape of a forest.
To welcome the ink, paper
will listen so carefully
the guest
remembers a season
in a distant homeland
then begins to speak
words so true, so essential
someone must write them.

Pilgrimage to a Gingko Tree

Two hundred years
is a long time to be standing
in the same place. I walked slowly
around the flashing koi in the murky pond.
It's the slender, healthy trees—
sturdy sycamores along the road
dropping their unshaven faces
at your feet, maples
writing elegant calligraphy
in the cobalt sky—good strong trees.
You notice the absence of age, of limbs
twisted by living. In Shukkein Garden,
the stinky nuts and colorful leaves
are swept away. Paths are grooved
from the attention of brooms whispering
  remember fish gills gasping for dust
  remember the sound steam makes
   rising from the body
The scene in this flaming place
burned into people
after the atomic bomb turned
everything to shadows or ashes.
Is this what you came to poetry for?
The gingko tree faced into the wind
and stood against the blast. Still,
you can sit under its thick arms
and catch a flash of sunlight
in a porcelain blue sky.

Crossing Motoyasu Bridge

Blue river, white granite.
Both smooth, both peaceful.
Rebuilt to look like itself,
the bridge leads directly

to a town gone. Blue sky.
White dove, the only one
I see in the flock. *This one,*
the man says, *pecked my hand open.*

All day I see
no blood, and all day
I find
no rest.

In the shallow pool,
gold koi, a small crab.
When they dug this pond,
the workmen wept to find

so many people's remains.
And so the fire continues
to burn. And the bridge
continues to stand.

Delta

Thus Hiroshima became a military city.
—from the Hiroshima Peace Reader

Not years, not a necklace
beaded with untouchable events,
it's a matter of deltas,
of the river's many mouths
and the songs they sing, the stories
held in mud and water. In Hiroshima,
in the mingling
of river with sea, you can hear
the father's tears denied,
even after so many years have blown away.

Streetcars rumbled to the end of the line
pouring forth more soldiers, more families
being torn apart. People were singing, swelling the port
with something that might hold them together
in this great and constant disintegration.

One father knows the sorrow
of neighbors: this one lost both sons,
that one their daughter to the factories.
He knows he won't see his boy again.
His weeping is Confucian weakness,
the selfish love
of a father for his son, a terrible force
in a nation chewing itself to death.
But when the soldier charges him,
the father claims his tears are pride.
Not every parent can give the nation
a warrior at such a critical time.

So tears and soldiers flowed
like the waters of the Ota River
into the island-dotted Seto Sea
and even today they sing that sadness.

Tides return to cover mudflats, floating
fishing boats moored to banks and bridges.
The water goes gray in rain to silver
in sunlight, sharp as any parents' pain.
The stories are hidden in the shells

of oysters and in the round suckers
on the many arms of the octopus.

Despite the books, war didn't end
with the rising of the sun-bright flash.
And the history of peace didn't then begin.
Something changed, that's certain,
but as long as brute power's blind stalking
goes on, peace by fear is no peace at all.
It's the same order as the days when those families
whose names ink the books of history
converged on this wide set of islands:
war was averted when one clan chose
to behead three of its leaders. They offered
this grisly concession at a Temple
where a golden Buddha holds his hands
in a reflective position. Meanwhile,

Hiroshima became a military city and
workmen began building the castle
that would house the Emperor
as he directed the war in Russia
(the foundation of which you can still visit,
though it's just stones in a city of stones
along a river in a city of rivers). Meanwhile,

regular people continued to seek the sea
and its treasures, women sunk their legs
in the rich delta soil, risking leeches
and murderous mosquitoes, to plant
tender rice shoots hoping to feed
their ever-growing families, singing

the song their mothers hummed as they planted,
not knowing the fate that awaited the sons of their daughters
and the daughters of their sons.

Gingko

—for Beth

All its family gone, this lonely one is left yearning for mates, females dropping fruit, males pouring out pollen. Along the moss-railed pathways of Sandankyo Gorge where the Ota is a single river, a single twisting thread held taut by ancient rocks, along this play of solid shapes and shifting voices, a single gingko sapling raises its thin arms. A Byzantine cross—small beam for the head, longer one for the outstretched arms. A living fossil. A lone descendant. A maiden letting her soft hair fall into the cold arms of autumn. Near this small tree which seemed to glow a buttery gold, near a small shrine with its stone Buddha wrapped in burning red, I picked up a gingko leaf. Tiny tributaries crash out of the hard rock of lost ages, spread out, reaching. Soft as your cheek, both now and at the time of first desire, soft as that moment when our words fall like dry and empty hulls, when all that can communicate is touch, a tired hand reaching for the lover's face.

Tancho (Cranes)

I now feel from the bottom of my heart that the "barrenness" of that place has been a blessing of nature, since its unwelcome qualities as far as humans are concerned are precisely what keep the habitat of the tancho intact.
—writer and photographer Masahiro Wada

— 1 —

A box of snow
in a day of sun
A wall of irises
in a life of love
A page of cranes
in the book of sky

In the feather of a crane
there is no anger no desire
In the shape of a grain of corn
there is no anger no desire
In the slope of a snowfield
In the tongues of flowers
In the bitterness of these marshes
there is no desire no anger

— 2 —

This hardship this particular
trial scatters
only a handful of corn

It is enough   though   to live on
It is enough to tip back my head
and call to the snow-heavy clouds

It is enough
to flap my wings and dance
for the sake of my love

from
THE METAL OF MY MOUTH

(FootHills Publishing, 2004, Poets on Peace #7)

Why I Think About Hiroshima & Nagasaki

I'm happy. I've got
plenty to eat.

Pumpkins cooked
in their shells; potatoes baked
under the hot dirt.

I wasn't alive, so I
don't remember.
1945. War.

"He took a woman by the hands
but her skin...

Look at these hands,
they have plenty of fingers.

her skin slipped off
in huge, glovelike pieces."

My life is good.
Tony Medwid showed me
a roofing tile from an old
Catholic cathedral—the largest
in Asia. It was ruined
by the atomic bomb.

Another woman huddled herself
around her child—dead
for four days.

The clay tile
had bubbled in the heat.
Boiled.

She held that baby
even after the body
had begun to decay.

"Imagine," he said,
"what would happen
to the human body."

The Missing

Everything everything comes back   returns
to the deaths the deaths   missing
Everything will be all right   Will everything
Don't worry   Try to get some sleep
How can we sleep   When everything
comes back will it have its place
It turns on a gap   empty gap
the desk empty   space on the elevator everything
comes back to the deaths the silences
holes in sentences in language   the deaths
holes in newspapers where photos go
where photos   where go   gaps
talk in the family   the bedroom
empty   the bed straight and neat
Will everything be all right   Will everything
sleep when it returns from death   Is there a quilt
in the empty bedroom   trophies   shoes
in the closet   Is there a silence
where words used to move   water
dripping water in the sink
the faucet dripping words   tapping stainless steel
words   bedrooms   closets   shirts   elevators
desks   shoes   newspapers   silence
everything comes back   Will everything
be all right   Don't worry

Times Like These

I think it better that in times like these
A poet's mouth be silent, for in truth
We have no gift to set a statesman right...
  —Yeats, "On being asked for a War Poem"

His voice is electric, crackling
in waves from Washington to London,
from Baghdad to Beijing.
Metal and buzzing.
               The statesman
opens his mouth and people
turn to shadows
               on bank steps—
as Blake said,
'And the hapless soldier's sigh
Runs in blood down palace walls.'

Sand, dust, and skin flaking off in rafts
fill the air, cloud airways, stick
in thick mouths until voices rasp,
whisper, and go mute.
                    And so,
before my silence is enforced,
I raise my voice, offer what gift,
no matter what it does to the statesman.
               I
    must be made
               more human.
Silence
     is for stones.

Passing-bell

What passing-bell for these who die as cattle?
Only the monstrous anger of the guns.
   —Wilfred Owen "Anthem for Doomed Youth"

Under the weight of misty streets and lights
I say   I do not believe
I will not obey   Others will but
I will not follow into the dark neighborhood
My name has been forgotten   all our names

I cannot contain my rage   It spills out
It runs down streets   streets dark as polished marble
Streets closed in like hospital halls
My rage etches names in the night   My rage
catches like orders in my throat like curses
But stops   choking   I know I am not innocent

But I will not stop my anger

I am a bell   the metal of my mouth rings
it rings like sign faces hit with a fist
it rings like hubcaps pelted with stones
there are so many ways to die   I am a bell

the heavy clapper swings

a bell's weight   cannot be measured   its weight
is darkness   darkness   dense as absence
dark as closed malls   dark like the shadows
under bridges   dark as mouths
mouths open to the night   open in rage
rage etching names into the night   rage
etching all our names into solid night

Like Superman

I know I'm just flapping my arms here,
he said, but I don't want no parts
of any turkey shoot. He said

he used to dream of flying, not in planes,
but walking down the neighborhood,
taking a few steps and actually

lifting off. Like Superman, he said,
like Superman. I never wanted to be
in the Air Force, his voice getting small

in a cell somewhere in Germany.
Now Rob wants another war
so he can go, and a woman in the room says,

when you get on TV, don't be boring.
We don't want our wars
boring, our press conferences dull,

our generals too mundane. We want
soldiers who can describe the action
like sports announcers. "It's like," they say,

"It's like a turkey shoot." All those birds
flapping their useless wings. These people
can't fly F-15s, and they can't

run away fast enough. So he sits in his cell
somewhere far from the journalists' pool,
bored, waiting for the military court

to accuse him of not killing anyone.

Something about Peace

Green as pondskin,
the tray carries a lily
in its shape. A brown leaf
tells of autumn. Birds
—folded gold, yellow,
blue like a piece of sky—
say something about peace,
something we must carry
in our hands to understand.

from

THE LUMINOUS HOUSE

(Finishing Line Press, 2007)

Art does not reproduce the visible, rather it makes visible.
Formerly, we used to represent things visible on earth,
things we either like to look at or would have liked to see.

Today we reveal the reality that is behind these visible things...

—Paul Klee

Coming to Bloom

In the ground, the strongest,
most reliable color is sleep.

Coming to bloom means, after
long standing and irregular aches,

quantum growth. The nobility
of starlight comes to earth,

the radiance of heaven
is *now*. The moon's tidal rhythms

teach persistence
teach *you-just-wait.*

Joyful and true, the moon
hums its own dark song.

Cold slows tempos down.
Winter means *rest a while*

it means *prepare, prepare,*
something great is becoming,

but for the moment
snow is the color of hope.

Ancient Sound (1)

bare trees   leaves all blown into snow   trees
all branches and clouds   leaves like a name

when they sprout   we read Emphysema and Malaria
Malnutrition Stroke   all tomorrows are leaves

what's the word for cancer spreading to the marrow
it's all now and now   birds and light   all returning

March   the heart stripped   all stark outline
a bare sycamore   a bone white elegy

maybe you hear it   have heard it
but now   now you're ready

below incident   below the crash of circumstance
the faithful hum   the constant song

the earth sounds through   and death
has no place in it   step down and tune yourself

Dance of the Mournful Child

On her cheek, she wears an umbrella
half open, always ready.
She may be small
but can expand when she spins
tilting her head.

The world isn't what we expected
in the awful architecture of history,
that house of shame
where Nazis live just downstairs
(never left, never leave).

She may be young but already
bears the imprint of brutality,
knows in every age some
will slaughter for a vision.

So she tips up on her toes,
and with outstretched arms
counters gravity.
Through her feather
she looks inward, looks outward
and does the dance
her mother taught, mother dance
of sorrow, mother dance of loss.

Mr. Z

cannot sleep. His mind is orange,
cheeks red. All night
he rehearses embarrassment.
Words spoken, words withheld.
His head expands with shame,
eyes reduce to slits.

Come morning, dawn's steady hand
watercolors the sky again,
but Mr. Z will watch his feet.
He cannot tell
whom he'll let down today.

> *a reptile*
> *curled in the belly*
> *shame meters us*
> *by the rule*
> *in others' eyes*
> *sometimes there*
> *sometimes no*

Soon, it is dusk,
time of many landscapes,
when trees flame, mapping
all the directions. Up, down,
inside, out. Now and now.

Mr. Z

can't believe how grizzled he got
in just one night. The task of shaving
grows heavier because he's so tired,
eyes like flags at half-staff,
weary with mourning.

Everything the Nazis did,
he says to the still-foggy mirror,
was legal. Lawfully elected,
they followed their rules religiously
right to the end of the train line.

He wavers a little with correction
then decides there's more
on the compass-face, more cardinal points
than *victim* and *executioner*.
In the reflective silver square,

he shaves himself smooth,
puts on his best face to join
his fellow citizens,
neighbors, countrymen,
in the maze that is Market Street,

determined to search out
those who'd shelter a family in the attic.
Faces will not betray
such righteous nobility—
smooth is as smooth does.

Full Moon

If you draw a line from the lemon tree,
the fish-bone tree, the upright prayer,
the pleased-to-be element

and connect it to the town square
you'd pass right through an open window,
black night divided in four.

The light of this full moon
casts vermillion shadows
from any solid thing. Inside,

through drawn curtains, wind
runs its slender fingers, their green nature
will not let it stay long. What grace,

what loveliness is sheltered,
shuttered, there? A movie camera
would pan the wool rug's

pattern of wear, the wall photos
grouped from sandbox giggles
to bespeckled school portraits,

from the wedding picture, sunglare
making bride and groom squint
as they wave over the rented car,

to sleepy parents in hospital gowns,
the baby red-faced and amphibious,
to new playgrounds, new portraits...

From this opening sequence, we're given
to understand the person, one life's
treasured net of influences, and so feel,

really feel the losses sure to come
as the plot unreels. But this is no film.
We are able to stare at this full moon

until faces emerge everywhere
to stare back so that we can draw
our own lines, our own lives:

in our chock-a-block town,
a lit checkerboard of magic squares,
there is always a tree to start from.

Love Song by the New Moon

In the moon's unreflected light, gray
is the color of our becoming:
love and death, longing and being forgotten,

the silver feather earring lost in snow
is discovered again in mud-time.
The oldest, most faithful melody,

the song of the earth cycles
and repeats so nothing's
ever lost—snow is the child's squeal leaping

in summer over foamy ocean-swells.
Each person's a moon in phase,
breath full, breath new.

Each person's heart is a lacquered box
and in that box is a string of yeses.
May we put them on in the end.
May we wear them when the timeless comes.

In the moon's unreflected face
is the song of the earth,
its final refrain we finally join:
harmony of love, harmony of being.

Ancient Sound (II)

how can elegy touch us   here how
in June's jade   all is vibrant

we wear ourselves out   with foliage
crowded viridescent   all is verdant

we breathe its vegetable breath
trees flame green   how can sadness

reach us here   conscience shades
hayfields of shame   emerald pea olive

in mansions of regret   we learn to live
in compromised rooms   closed chambers

in ourselves   begin with mourning
the losses you cause   the losses you are

begin with sadness   the dance
you know you know   the dance of mourning

shake the shame of being   what is
is   and will not be coaxed into nothing

you are we are   the song of moonlight
its green glow and slow hum

you are we are   the sap of the earth
its green glow and slow hum

we are you know the nobility of becoming
its green glow   its slow and faithful hum

This Star Teaches Bending

Though long, night was not finished
and not finished with him. He stands,
arms outstretched to lean
against the windowframe, peering
into a gauze of darkness.

In sleep Mr. Z traveled long, clanging
high-school locker-gauntlets
to the house of his first girlfriend
where she's raising children
he never knew about
with a man he never met.
At the door, arms lengthening
with the weight of his luggage,
he is afraid she will kiss him.
Instead, she says, *Find out if angels*
molt like we do. If anyone
can tell me, you can.
Then, she presses into his hand
a subway token, a blue jay feather.

Then he sees it on the snow,
laying heavily and circled by deer tracks.
It is such a wide orbit we ride
and gravity's draw is not the only pull.
Something beyond us, something
we cannot seem to bear attracts us.
This he understands
because his heart has red-shifted,
a knot has softened and may be worked.

So he goes out to examine the animal tracks,
a series of hollows, crossing.

Today it has come to him.

Mr. Z hefts the star, hunching
under it, strapping it to his back.
moving slowly and with great care—
to become a star carrier.

The Forgetful Angel

When he opens his wings, desert sand,
pigeon feathers, the scent of funeral smoke
and sandalwood shakes loose.
His man, in ICU with a wound
like a polluted river down his chest,
wandered snowy spirit-fields alone
before this angel appeared on the scene.

Once in Hiroshima's Peace Park, that green wedge,
that seared arrowhead of history,
this angel sat under cherry blossoms
while salarymen drank sake and beer.
The smile on his plaintive face
was almost enough to make you take root.

Mostly, the Forgetful Angel arrives late,
apologizing to high heaven, then hangs back
or gets pushed behind the caution tape
like an ordinary onlooker.

It's a question of devotion, really,
not obedience: in an alley in Philly
where steam grates issue wavering ghosts,
amid ruin stink and dumpster spillage,

he is the witness that stays,
hovering long after his shift,
hovering over the cardboard,
hovering before the ascent.

Mr. Z

remembers the long hours after school
how he'd stand at the easel, toothy paper
filling—lines in loops and fiery blooms,
paint in smears, layering on.
He knows he needs to lose himself like that,
to dissolve into time. Mr. Z knows
what he needs:

the Tibetan monks, their throaty song,
many voices from a single mouth,
chanting chanting
all the way to the river
where the colored sand poured away.

He knows he is no painter
but is authoring his own life.

Critics in, critics out.
Those nibblers, those doubters:
finding fault doesn't mean
being right.

Tired of the shame he supposes
others assign him, he shifts his allegiance.

Mr. Z knows what we have
(though you can't see it yet).
Soon his back will be straight.
From his astonished body—
a glow, something warm,
something colorful.

The Light and So Much Else

I wear myself out with looking, eyes
weary of lines undrawn, colors unblended,
signs changing meaning, unknowns beyond count,

but still the light drenches us, washing
over in waves, coating us in tiny fragments,
sun and moon sharing our one sky.

This is the sound of love, whisper of possibility,
a sigh like sheets of paper sliding one
atop the other, their angles opening

in us whole new vistas, a view of interiors,
steps ascending, the descent beckoning.
The song of becoming repeats in us

in the pattern of a cardinal's flight,
in the long blue line of the horizon,
in the flutter of a pennant that begs

no loyalty. I wear myself
like a multi-colored coat, square upon square
of light and hue, spirit and more.

from
PILGRIMAGE TO A GINGKO TREE

(WordTech Communications, 2008)

Another Journey

I am very happy to begin a new journey to faraway places
by means of the brush in my mouth.
        —Tomihiro Hoshino

Even Basho wandered all over the island
plucking haiku and stringing them
like wisteria through his books. But you,

you must sit. And stare. Silent and intent,
your mouth is a vast meditation hall,
How can it possibly keep pace
with this microchip world?

I heard that a temple in Kyoto
has a zendo floor so polished
when you bow, you see yourself.

Broken: you begin.
Motionless: you travel.
Empty: you gather.

In the Shadow of Shirakiyama

All afternoon the moon
ploughed the watery fields
of the day-blue sky,

and now glows white
over blushing hills.
Yellow flowers on tall stalks

stand like lanterns
above thinning rice fields.
The muddy soil, stuck

with harvest-stubble, darkens
until night, like rice, rises
up from the earth.

Origami

Folded by an old woman, silver bird
what do you know? Your paper feathers
are slippery. You give the light back.

At the flash she dropped like a rag.
A single day, a single bird: the day
that repeats itself with each crease.

The hours stretch out like crows' wings.
Samuel said he wanted to come here
to help people forget the past. My eyes burn

with the day's unrelenting length.
My life is brief and my sight short.
No wonder she keeps turning paper
in her creased but unburned hands.

Cosmos

Here you can follow a river
into the mouth of the Buddha,
enter its benevolent darkness
then emerge again at the sea.
The word *no* is so common
even I recognize its lovely
spiral back through centuries.
Here *no* can be possessive.
And many are surprised
that the word *cosmos*
means the same thing.
Are these just games with words
or am I saying anything
useful? What can I say
to a twelve-year-old girl
who reaches for the sky?
At the end of her finger,
the size of her thumbnail,
a comma drops
from the belly of a plane,
and for the rest of her life
she says, "No," firmly,
flatly, over and over
to anyone who will listen.

Aioi

What does it take
to lift a bridge?

One woman volunteered
to search the still-burning city
for neighbors and relatives
but couldn't put her foot
on the surface of the bridge—

How does it feel to walk
on people? I can only repeat

what I've been told. The bomb
exploded in the air

to spread its arms wider.

The river water bowed down
and returned to itself.

This bridge
arched into the hot air
only to settle again,
a new thing.

All Burning

—for Sumiko Izawa

                She folded herself
into a small package, legs and feet
under her body, words
even smaller.
                In a language
I don't understand, she tells us
about parents, about their small,
folded children all burning,
red-orange and pink.
Of course, somewhere in all this
there is a flag.
                You could say
her voice is like a bird on a thin wire
in strong wind—
she tells us
                this story,
I've made this story thousands of times.
What happens to a person
who must carry such words,
fold them smaller,
                each day,
                        smaller?
What must happen
                when they
                        fly away?

The Night Cafe

after van Gogh

Others drink until their heads
knock the tabletop;
I'm ruining myself

counting red. The lines
in the points of my eyes,
poppies wagging

their heads in the fields,
a frame limiting
a perfect Japanese print.

The doves' amber eyes
do not count,
so when they fly off

I begin again.
And when they land
on a bridge in Hiroshima

that's enough of red.

Harvest Moon-viewing

The moon slips under the bridge
where the line of orange rowboats can't reach.

Warm and close, two lovers on the riverbank
throw stones into dark water.

All eyes are on the moon tonight.

A rough bundle of a woman
gathers plastic bags against the cold

then is so motionless

she could be a whole town asleep
or dead and gone these many years.

The moon sleeps quietly on the water.

The Bridge

after Monet

The green and flowering
water steps down three times.

Willows listen,
their fine tips descending.

Uncurling like seahorses,
the ferns grow outward
in ways greed can never know.

Above all this, the bridge.

Defying water, defying earth,
it joins them both
to air. And my efforts,

like pollen,
are nearly weightless.

At the Calligraphy Festival

The woven mats
are like grass underfoot.
The stairs lead to airy rooms
where the sound of wings is so quiet
I almost cannot hear it. There
a tiger hides in the sunset.
A mouse hides in the leaves.
A man dangling from the end of his rope
tastes honey. An ancient story
hides in the frayed end of a stick,
in the hair of a goat,
in the feathers of a quail.

Blocks of ink pressed with a seal.

An inkstone so black
the ink
disappears.

In a quiet room,
a woman is learning to write her name;
the bristles are a collection of refugees
heading down a white road
leaving a black trail behind.

On one scroll
the characters are so finely drawn
they look like birds
flying away for the winter.

> —*Kumano*

Passing

What will you miss
that moment when everything
untangles, soul from sinew?
Tell me, wanderer,
who are you before you think
your thoughts and before
you feel your feelings?
You will pass quietly through
the cell of sleep, the eyes
of the sea. Tell me how much
will all your goals and regrets
weigh when you float
into the blue heart of the flame?

Sandankyo

— 1 —

Out of the green legends
in Japan's ancient rocks,

white water spills itself
into autumn-chilled air.

One sister has no name
so the other two

do all the talking,
falling all the way

to the word-weary pool
made clear by silence.

— 2 —

Rocks, cut
like steps. Water,
cold as fear.
How can I pass

without thinking
how short
life is? Red rocks
and laughing water.

The Sower

after van Gogh

Under a splintering sun
I throw handful
by desperate handful
what I have

into blue fields.
Crows break in—they
are not my enemy
though they take

all color into themselves.
This paced earth
is my living. I give it
everything I have.

from
PART DARKNESS, PART BREATH

(Plain View Press, 2008)

Into Darkness

—1— Descent

Sometimes when I am breathing carefully, not taking for granted the complexities of that filling and emptying, how molecule by invisible molecule I touch the cottonwood tree quivering in the breeze, sometimes I feel a descent. I sink into an image of darkness. I descend into soil. *God saw that the light was good and God separated the light from the darkness* because *darkness was already with God.* Like breath, it didn't need to be created—both were in God before the beginning. My breathing is sometimes like this, a trail I follow, a river path after flash flooding: willow and brush all tangled and crossed, all pointing in the direction of water's flow. I follow this breathing, this thin strand that comes out of my body and connects me to the world. I think of Beth's cornflower seeds, which breathe even in the dark of their packets at the store. Though they need light, the seeds would burn up if we threw them into the sun, but hidden in the soil, separated from the light, they sprout. They emerge like hands, heels together, palms up ready to catch moisture, sunshine, and the whole breathing world, and funnel it down into the roots, just beginning to reach out. Sometimes when I am breathing carefully, this is what I am.

—2— *Only This*

In the beginning there was no time
and nothing to measure it with
there was only this

Darkness closed in around itself
wonderful and perfect

In the darkness there was breathing
it moved through the dark
part darkness and part breath

In the breathing there were waters
over which the breath moved

In the waters there was no violence
as creation had not begun
there was motion but no matter

In the beginning there was radiation
moving in all directions at once

—3— On the Trinity

"The effects could be called
unprecedented,
magnificent, beautiful, stupendous,

and terrifying. The whole country
was lighted by a searing light
with the intensity many times
that of the midday sun. It was golden,

purple, violet, gray, and blue.

First the air blast pressed hard against people,
to be followed almost immediately
by the strong, sustained awesome

roar which warned of doomsday

and made us feel we puny things
were blasphemous
to dare tamper with the forces

heretofore reserved for the Almighty."

(General Farrell, Deputy to Manhattan Project Commander
General Leslie Groves: On the Trinity Test, July 16, 1945)

The Maple Leaf Elegy

You walk out into startling sunlight,
into shadowed breezes and the sound of water
riding into air and falling again to water,
you stand stunned, in the fire
      and division of a broken age,

in an age of war and preparing for war,
an age like any other, when children
learn to count and sing the alphabet
and expect all that life offers
      in its ripening and falling to earth,

the embrace of earth, the tether of it
on our daily dreams. You catch yourself
in the motion of a falling maple leaf,
its red sharpness, its butterfly flight,
      its rest and final comfort.

For once comforted by these limits, freed
and energized, you now expect your own
temporary and sweet ordinariness.
You expect the sound of water in autumn
      to bring you to tears.

Fishing Boats on the Beach

after van Gogh

Crimson like roses. Like our lives,
they are outlined in black, deep and impenetrable.
Blue oars to dip into water
when winds fail. Like the sun
crowning the horizon, these boats
carry such promise. They seem to smile,
filled with something that settles them
into the sand. I think of Jesus

in the tossing prow
while wild animals took up the shape
of the sea. He said his friends
were of little faith, believing so much
in the logic of nature,
of what is most visible.

He rose, spoke to the water and wind,
and they lay down to sleep,
contented. Night gathered around the boat,
leaving the men to wonder
which promise to believe.

First Frost

The sun covers the red wall,
descends slowly, row of bricks
by row, each brightening, almost
glowing. I am going to be late.
A weight within slows me.
Outside, few leaves are left green;
colors flash in the light,
in the wind that wakes me.
I hurry up the wood-chip path
where last week's storm—
with the suddenness
and brief power of a summer rain—
streamed some of the mulch away
revealing mud underneath. There, today,
on the dark earth worn smooth:
an intricate design of ice,
a white map, spread flat on the ground.
No placenames, no knobs of towns,
only lines, connecting one way
with another, visible in long light
of an autumn morning. As more
make their way into the swirling
world, even this thin map
will melt away, leaving only
the earth we walk on, the wind
we move through, and the light.

Bedrock

I lie on my back on rock that saw
the scrape of glaciers, the long history
of water carrying away layer after soft layer
until this barren bed faced the air.
No water runs now on this side of the stream,
only sky and wind in their dry currents.

I wear boots I thought durable,
a purchase I agonized over.
They carried me though deserts
and across alkaline plains, down a path
edged by ferns and redwoods
to the rocky beach
and the vast, mothering sea.

Now hundreds of miles
from any ocean, in a canyon
cut by water which still runs
in its course, here I lie:
small as the droplets that float out
invisibly from the great falls,
an itch, a breath,
a wink in the eye of stone.

Walking Meditation

Although we walk all the time, our walking is usually more like running.
When we walk like that, we print anxiety and sorrow on the earth.
—Thich Nhat Hanh

—i—

A wind this sharp this
studded should be
illegal   In some places
it is   They drive up
in black cars yank you in
and take you away

Or they roll
dark windows down and gun
across the whole crowd

You know this   You know
the electrodes to the earlobes
the genitals   *Peace* you say
is every step   You know

the danger
is not only outside
in the street
The threat must
begin somewhere

Peace is every step

—ii—

As if the tender one   her lover
were the blade   he ran
the knife along her skin
scratching the bumps of spine
the blue map of veins
along her wrist   her throat

He pressed it against her
until the metal
was no longer cold

He'd gotten in easily   as easily
as the man who broke the window

of an 84-year-old West Toledo woman
That one stole a ten and five ones
from the old woman's purse
after raping her

—iii—

Vietnam is only as far away
as your name   I like how breath
begins your name
and silence

completes it   Both
have the same shape

I like how delight
and discovery
run naked in the streets

—iv—

Before turning the video camera on
she testified

her husband
dragged her by the throat
into the bedroom   taped her mouth and eyes shut

No her husband answered
I didn't rape my wife   How
can you rape
your own wife

—v—

This bitter wind should be outlawed
Now that the pumpkin
wears a white cap of snow   I walk

Cut across backyards   between neighbors'
up the brick street
                —I'm almost running—
usually have to wait for the light at Main   then either
across the still-carless parking lot   or straight up
to Saint Aloysius Church and grade school
and angle across the playground   There

I step across the world

—vi—

Where do we start
Like you we are monks
shut up   in our little worlds
of striving

Awareness
What do you mean
Awareness

Could you explain please

Awareness   awareness   awareness

—vii—

In any of the houses on Clough
Prospect   Summit   Railroad
she could slide back
the glass door   step quietly
down a few concrete stairs

Each meeting of foot
with ground   a terror

—viii—

With the war walking freely
harrowing the fields the villages the people
children grew up   used to it
We learn to think violence
is the only way

The holy ones of your monastery decided to leave
decided to walk out of those Buddhist walls

You learned a new way
of awareness   another way
of compassion   No
it didn't stop the killing

You stepped into the war
and took the broken bodies in your arms

because peace
because healing

because

it is the only way
to begin

Story

The room was not crowded; people scattered
in the folding chairs in twos and threes.
Anne Coleman shied from the microphone,
but took it and told about her daughter,
Frances, dead eleven years, told
about the overworked and therefore
callous police—a process, she said,
that created not justice but rage,
a blue and burning rage. They could give
only four days to each case
with all the other murders going on.

The killer was never caught.
Some shook their heads at this.
The stillness was complete listening.

The wellspring of anger continued
to bubble up in their lives
until it consumed her son.
Two years after his sister's funeral,
Daniel killed himself. Some of us
wept, but Anne Coleman was done
with tears. She continued to tell.
And all the while this story
of sorrow was carving a space
in us. Even as we gained details
and understanding, something
slipped out of us with the current.

Years later, she met another mother
whose son was about to die. "The State,"
Anne told us, "was deliberately
going to kill in my name."
She knew the absence in the heart,
the gap in the family,
about to be created, she knew
the rage, so she visited every inmate
on death row, she wore placards
to stop the killing. She—
who'd lost so much—asked us
to acknowledge our place

"in the chain of violence."

And now when I hear
words like *murder* or *vengeance,*
but especially *forgiveness*
that space hollowed out
by this story suddenly
     and completely
         fills up

and the story begins to move

like an animal
     roused from sleep.

Almost

*If someone had told us then
you would die in nineteen years,
would it have sounded
like almost enough time?*
—Donald Hall *"Letter in the New Year"*

Seeing a tuft of fur on the highway shoulder
—brick-red, brown, blackened by oil
and sun—struck me wordless, numb.
An appropriate hollowness
had filled the morning, growing as heat
spread into shade. Somehow,
without knowing when
or how, we had opened the door
to death and now it inhabits us.
Your colleague's husband. Genevieve
killed at noon by a drunk driver.
The birds we draw to feeders, one's head
picked to a small, white ball.
Even the kitten we adopted
from the dairy farmer. Grief eroded me
in ways I never knew, so I tried to reason:
She was just an animal
      —as if you are anything else.
We knew it was coming
      —who wrote 'our steps are brief'?
All we could do was fill ourselves
with cheap wine and the night
with talk of other encounters.
Death is a feast we can only take in portions.
Kitten, father, sister, grandfather, cousin.
You cried yourself to sleep
imagining being left without me.
All morning, I drove with the taste of loss
in my mouth until passing
a row of three Mountain Ash trees
with their orange fruit glowing in the light
—somehow the beauty of it
broke me. Tears salt-burned my eyes.
At lunch we held each other,
swaying in a hug that will not
last forever, not even in memory.

Fossil

The shell will leave a sign   Each layer
each day-worn worry   however slight
is a weight I wrestle under   struggling and rolling
in a slice of light the color of seawater

I resist the comfort of sleep   that quality of night
that redeems darkness   I am tearing
my heart out again   It takes a long time
for sleep to settle   like the sea shifting
in its tides   slowly laying sediment over the living

Abandoned by life   the shell
will leave its signature in stone   and I
in a seatide motion am alive

There is something constant in the drifting dark
Breathing with the slow rhythm of sleep
you have floated off   leaving your book
like a bird   hovering over you

The world was born   of water of the sea
and of necessity   learned to fly
to ride the motion of air   to breathe it directly

Passing Steve's Field

The fiddle began with the most obvious
before taking on the more difficult truths:
there is nothing to be afraid of.

The low spring sun was warm, laying
soft color along the yellow-budding hills.
On 228 between Alpine and Trumansburg
a field of ruined farm machines

took on a glow of achievement, of a job
done well, not only to work the land
but to mine it and shape its metals.
And now that it's accomplished,
the human labor can't bear the sun
in its May orbit. I've started calling it

Steve's Field because he first
drew my attention to its range of rusted beauty. Death
takes many avenues, and none of them
really quick; in the meantime,

there is music from Cape Breton Island,
the smile on Beth's face, head bobbing
to the music, and the way
love sometimes feels like a hillside
swaying in the sunset. The fiddle
proceeded to the slower, harder truths,
the more elusive ones, like renewal.
Going up to have dinner with Steve,
friendship was breaking open

in another dying American town.
And for weeks, we'd been feeling
our own germination, even as
we moved (again)
all our boxes of books and pottery and
cookware and all the other things
we only partly own
and are owned in part by.

By the time the fiddler moved out of the Air
and into the next section, we too ached with joy

as we hurtled down a New York sideroad:
we felt the thrill of a whole crowded hall
bursting into applause
as she began dancing as she played,
the music of another kind of spring.

Holder Of My Dreams

She holds the tiny dill seeds,
scatters them along the fence.

I want to make my life
a gesture like that. Together
"we are a multitude," just as Ovid said.

When she reads aloud
on car trips across states,
she does all the voices,

and I am happy with her
all along the way.

How Ants Felled Two Trees

Before the circling wind let loose
its hungry pack of dogs

Before the rain weighed everything down with grief

Before the upper-atmosphere currents
aligned themselves for acrimonious stillness

Before summer became what it is

There were ants

Black and numerous like drops of blood, like omens,
ants following the invisible trails
laid down by the bodies of their fellow ants
to the exposed heart of the sweetgum tree.

Each creature took only what it could bear,
no more and no less.

I don't know how the bark
was opened, but it was enough.

And before the ants,
before that engineered line of thieves,
there was a fragrance, a sweetness
going out into the world.

Nothing To Do With Decoration

for Mary Donald

The sea crumples
               and rises up

of it
   the pelican and hermit crab

With metal
           you can shape
your life into any form
                 except joy
That must soften
           of its own fire

Art-making
         like lovemaking
has nothing to do with
            accessories

It is soul-beauty
         and it is commitment
to live by it
       in things and in selves

Crafting their own
          sharp lives
barrel cactuses
       in the dry Texas hill country
flower by it

Grace Street

we are a multitude
—Ovid

where we prepare an empty house that stood hollow & quiet for months
    seeming to wait for us
where the sander stripped thresholds
    filling the air with wood-dust fine as pollen
where we unpack the mask of Tengu from his wooden box
    and set him to guard against evil
    hanging from the thermostat
where we live, and so we live, crowded together by passions

where, in the tired ease after work, we hear the doorframes
    how they remember the sound of a fist
    hitting a woman's face
where we join the doors in their resolve
    to receive such suffering
    and respond with hospitality
    and the stories feel it and come to warm themselves

where sparrows bring their hearty expectations
and co-workers find a scroll
    that answers a longing
    they can only weep to comprehend
where a friend's mother can leave like an offering
    one small, sharp detail from divorce
where a kitten lives and dies
    and is buried under green feathers
    and the wind's occasional song
    and the watchful eye of sunflowers
where a toad can tunnel a secret home in cedar mulch

where we shot darts at politicians on TV
    and they stuck, they stuck
where we share the same couch to watch a movie
    leaving the other furniture to fend for itself

where lies are not welcome
where a listening sometimes emerges
    like Don's Russian tomato plant in the compost
    and we hear a rustling
    and move forward with strange confidence

where the mockingbird casts handfuls of musical pebbles down the chimney
and the oriole spends a few weeks
    stringing garlands from the locust tree
    then leaves us silence for the summer where its song once was

from
EVERYDAY OBJECTS

(Plain View Press, 2015)

The Romantic Quest

Like hummingbirds
that buzz and whir in their quest
for sweetness, the extension cord

is on a romantic search for beauty.
It quietly crackles
when connecting that surge,

filled in an instant with
an awareness: *the burning oneness
of it all, and here I am*

*one small part, a loop
in the great coil, a type
for the universe itself.*

But in idle moments, wrapped
in an orderly circle or jumbled
at the bottom of the closet,

all electricity gone,
the extension cord is stunned
by doubts, a flock of *Yes*

but's. It's not enough to have
the experience and savor it,
it wants the meanings too.

The Bathtub

It strives to be empty, to open
itself to the limitless
out of which all things

emerge and back into which
they sink. The bathtub
(to make good use

of its idle hours) cultivates
an attitude of generosity
so that everything it gains

—water falling and filling,
steam swirling, then
the toe, the foot,

the whole naked body—
everything
it gives away again.

The tub tries
to let the world pass through
without clinging, without

wanting more,
but the ring, soap's
grey residue, betrays it.

Everyday Shames: Parenthood

The children watched TV
until their eyelids grew too heavy
and they slept where they sprawled.

Late dinner even for summer.
A kind of family reunion
so the table

was long on talk and laughter.
Then—*OK!*—time to go. Marci got Daniel,
Andy gathered up Michael—

both boys slouched, bodies
without resistance. I hesitated
over Elizabeth, unsure,

not afraid but unable to begin.
"Just pick her up...Here,
you want me to do it?"

Suddenly, with no children
and no aptitude for their care,
I am in high school again

wondering how the hallways
of my life will look, what steps
will lead me through them,

and what tests will fail me.

you do the math

three men check into a motel
and decide to share one room
the clerk tells them   *that's thirty dollars*
so each one puts up ten
and they all head upstairs

aren't we all swaying on that problematic train
which left Philadelphia or San Francisco
aren't we all passing through
variables   tangled in equations
where the duties of sons and daughters
are added to a pound of feathers
then divided and scattered over exposed earth
death is just another equal sign

remember the motel clerk   she startles to realize
the room costs twenty five not thirty bucks
so she sends the bellboy up
who shrewdly calculates
that five dollars won't divide evenly
among three   he pockets two
and gives each man a dollar refund

a man's mother tells him
if I am seventy three and I live
to be eighty five   and you visit
at this same rate well   you do the math

consider the elegance
of numbers   especially zero
that breakthrough of thought   the measure
for what is not here and maybe
never was

each man paid nine dollars   nine
times three is twenty seven
plus the two in the bellboy's pocket
equals twenty nine
where'd the other dollar go

Stuart Little, Yellow House, Avalon, NJ

Spotted from a winter's wind and rain,
the picture window stared up First Avenue.
One car all evening. Only the wind's moan,
surging and dying like waves. In April's dampness
the pebble lawn appeared mossy and yellow.

A week-out-of-school just Julie and I
and Mom preparing for Easter.
No television, and only Mom's music
on the black leather-cased radio
(folded paper wedging buttons down),

so we listened to warmed air hushing
through floor vents, and the wind
forcing rain across the island.
After finding faces in knotted paneling
we settled into the sofa. The picture window

had long since become a mirror
reflecting a sister and brother
listening to their mother's voice
over the constant rush of rain.

Thanksgiving

New light gathers slowly
in white mist. The bitter heart
of winter. Snow coats the yard
smoothing it down to the road then up again
to the field where cows grazed all autumn.
Now snow owns it all. Frost

in the lower corners of the window
webbed cold designs. Inside:
only piano music. And my breath
fogging the glass. I have been up all night.

Sparrows, quick as the wind,
dart into gaps in the wrought-iron railing.
It will not get much brighter today
or warmer; the cold light,
slow as frost, is enough.

Everyday Shames: Scouting

Florescent-lit basement.
Two half blocks of balsa wood
hollowed out for the rubber band engine.
They told me carve to a point,
so I did. I imagined a metallic streak
down the side of my flyer,
but painting's the finale, like cake
after dinner. First came carving
then sanding. When I was done,
I had a needle: silver balsa
sharp as failure with metal hooks
for the guide wire. Winding up
the plastic propeller, I crushed
the front cone. Delicately, I tried
to salvage it—worthless.
I twisted my work in my hands,
lumping it into beige and silver junk.
Tonight, everyone will be happy,
jumping in the air, rejoicing
over each others' creations
just like in the Cub Scouts'
Handbook drawings:
I pleaded my parents for more wood.

Not enough time for smoothness
or beauty, so I carved little,
leaving edges blunt, hulking,
to support the tautest rubber band.
Black and grey, bulky
as hatred. I made it, and I hated it.
When I got to the school cafeteria,
I couldn't wait to show off
my contempt for balsa and Cub Scouts
by bringing out my black brick demon.
Mrs. Springly, Den Mother, asked
if maybe I should have spent
a little more time on it. What's she know
about needle dreams and shame?
My opponent had made a slick,
pointy-nosed plane. Everyone chuckled

as I wound up my apparent
lack of effort, my failure,
and hooked it to the wire.
I wondered if I should have
let the band hang slack, so the thing
wouldn't even make it down the run,
but I didn't. It made it,
and I was done, defeated,
but feeling a little victory,
empty, light as balsa.

(With Roethke) In a Watery Drowse

*"I ask you: I beg you: bring to this task all the sweetness
of spirit you possess."*
— Theodore Roethke

—i—

The rain's coming, these days of change
when the sweet pea is a blank bulb
on its dried up cord but grass is still green;
calendula's still in flower but only the oak
has leaves and they hiss and whisper.
The rain and more is coming. These days
the darkness is nearly dark enough to see.

—ii—

I've been reading your gob songs
and greenhouse memories
for more than forty years,
so when I step my way through
some of my lines, I hear
your rhythms and see your images.
Thoughts I thought were new
turn up tendrilled and rooted
in yours. I savor the influence
of a stranger, this dialogue
all poets have with the dead.
Imagination's not bound
by time or limits of skin
so when I read of your penchant
for trench coats and gangsters
I understand again the deeper
lawlessness that regulates the heart,
how imagination resists
command, recoils and slinks off
down the darkening alley.

—iii—

Teeth against teeth, mechanical clouds
slip a gear and begin to clamp down.
The time of soft souls.
Time for disappointing fathers.

Time, therefore, to be gangsters, you say.
If they're going to outside us,
may as well play the part.
May as well, may as well.

Still the Michigan clouds
glower over the silty pond.
Vireo, vireo, that song,
that tenderness. Who needs it.

We're worthless, too.
This stringer of fish, old boy,
nobody will buy. No one
wants what we've got for sale.

—iv—

Who wants to feel? Who wants a rhythm
that holds the heart in this sensation of loss,
of straining skin? At the start of winter
when the cold's just coming on, light is still
in a pile of leaves. We know what approaches,
it's coming for us all. Who wants to feel
and hold in the heart this rhythm?

—v—

Gangster means I'm making it on my own,
means even my weakness you should fear.

I'm above the law and below the radar
so you don't know what I'm up to.

Gangster means control, means respect,
means I've-got-something-coming-to-me.

What I've got, says the gangster, you want,
so you better ask, and ask real nice.

—vi—

My father worked for thirty years
marketing IBM computers,
and his father sold cars,
passing on the wisdom
that we're all salesmen.
Men who never read poetry.

Even though I was a strange
sort of creature to him,
he wanted my happiness
to be true. He's gone now,
another relative I imagine
listening from beyond
the far field.

—vii—

The wind is green
and does not sleep.
It catches time
and won't let go.

The speech we make
is made again
—word into act,
word into motion—

as we ourselves
are being born again
(O, to be worthy)
into earth.

—viii—

Wind blew the river dry
until it ran in memory only.

We approach on our knees
time's cream-colored pages

and trust the winds
to swerve astray.

—ix—

Look, it's raining again. The evergreens
are slashed by its movement.
Don't take this wrong,

but we're all alone.
Blood, hands, tongue,
they're all we've got.

Unlike geese in flight,
the dead do not come back.
Even you, my imagined brother.

The clouds pull taut
their yellowy light.
On the glass, see my fog?

Breath goes out—
will we recognize it
when it circles back?

But you're never gone either.
I take your word
and feel the fern's curling,

watch the spiraling drift
of an oak leaf, and make them
my own soul's motion.

R5: The Paoli Local

The men still read newspapers.
Women slide in beside women.
More people wear earphones
becoming unapproachable
for directions or the time.
My father took this train
for years. From before I was born
he'd walk the six blocks
to the station
morning and evening. We kids
never met him halfway,
hanging on him, but would wait,
slowly gathering around the kitchen.
With a booming greeting,
the nightly chant: *What say, what say?*
he'd swing open the huge,
wooden door. The same door
that lopped the top off Michael's thumb.
The same door that yawned open
wide enough for me to stand in,
wide enough for the bells of Wayne
to rush through. *The war is over,*
I was told.
We'd been fighting
longer than you've been alive.
I'd seen some things
on TV: helicopters, people
hanging onto the runners,
mobs of different-looking people.
But no one told me
if we'd won this war
I didn't even know we'd been fighting.

The Display Models

Most shoes sleep like rocks.
Tossed in a corner, they doze
where they drop, almost
on contact. But some,

troubled by the past,
carry a sorrow
they never speak of.

They recall the brief,
strange solitude, the ease
of those days, alone
on the small platform,
and the view of the world
they never have again.

Insomniac shoes—
they allow the long hours
to open themselves.
If they drop off, each creak
and rustle startles them awake.

They listen to the house
shift its heavy weight.
All night, they consider
what light inevitably reveals.

The Discontent of Everyday Objects

Under the great sodium streetlamps
and in the yellow pollen of their light,
surrounded by cars
all facing each other like line dancers,

I begin to understand
the discontent of everyday objects,
why socks are so devout
in their sadness, how the latch
in the car door grits its teeth and curses
every time it opens its mouth.

I stride into the vaulted mall
where fountains try to hoard
their coins, hiding them
like the children they never had,
but losing them,
they drown their sorrows in public.

The huge, never-blinking walls of glass
keep their complaints
to themselves. Behind them,
in clothing stores, on racks of shirts
all gathered in circles
and on the long dresses waiting in line
one behind the other—
all those zippers and snaps
argue about God
to justify their own existence.

And at the cooking store,
plastic food containers
stand around dreaming
of taking center stage but instead
are stuck in this dead-end job.

At the notions and fabric shop,
the tiers of homeless buttons
are too pitiful to even look at—
I can't even go near
the Dollar Store. I turn away,

walk on to the Bath and Body Boutique
where the prostitute lotions
long to settle down someday
and the scented soaps
are piled like stones,

or skulls, evidence
of a massacre only read about
in a country so far away
it might be a fantasy.

To One Born in a Time of Crisis

for Michael

The night kitchen here is quiet,
house calm enough to hear wind
growl in the chimney
like a trapped animal. As the chill
of early autumn descends,
there's nothing like a nice cup of tea
(as Mom put it) to warm hands,
mouth, chest. When she was just swelling with you,
the Bay of Pigs must have made
those April afternoons desperate.
Then, a year after you were born, missiles arrived
in America's backyard. Nevertheless,
benign and singular, the sun rose
over our childhood home outside Philadelphia,
the City of Brotherly Love.
The creek stones of the grotto
by St. Katharine's held firm.
There's a picture of us sitting on them:
you in a gold jacket, me
...I don't know about me,
I've lost the photo. We were in Wayne,
in wartime. Little of Vietnam
touched us, born when we were, late enough
to celebrate your fortieth birthday
in the televised shadow
of Manhattan's black smoke.
That terrible Tuesday, away from the news
I was busy with the details of my chosen life
—as we all were, I guess—but you were also
fingering the beads of a new decade.
If a Buddhist friend is right,
you've entered the time of wisdom.
When your oldest son asks why
people sleep under the dirt, do you feel
any wiser? Is life
mostly an approach to Calvary,
reward and joy to come later?
How did Mom get dinner together

for six kids—and you, just an infant—
when missiles
could have been humming north? Who knows
right now what brutalities
one person is pressing on another.
Who knows what's about to land.
Can we mention grace, or does that
dissolve responsibility
like sugar in a cup of tea?
In the grotto, the statue of Mary
was replaced or refurbished,
I remember her chipped face
and its worn-out look,
I remember her wide-armed,
constant embrace.

The History of Love

History takes its first breath long before
any record of it. In the beginning,
love was remote, without access,

without direction. In that time, a man ran
in leather dress shoes across a beach
with a vision as religious

as he was not, a message
for his confused buddy, my father.
Had he not been successful

our story would have been dust,
wind-blown. In that place, war
ate its young; the people

(through tears and patriotic songs)
were once again convinced
the unspeakable

was necessary. Meanwhile,
another young man, this one
with his bold moustache,

traveled in official olive greens
on trains, buses, and a ship
that traced an entire ocean

to a land he'd cry about
even as an old man, a land
where women giggled so easily

he became a jokester, where hunger
whittled children to ghosts
haunting him to his death.

War is this way, life
being so singular. And love,
like the past, processes before us

heading God-knows-where, through whatever
Promised Land as we are: and here
I find myself, insignificant I,

among all these forces, arriving
in winter to a midwestern
American town, when ice

coated the maples above Buttonwood,
glittering under amber clouds.
Here I'm granted citizenship

in your embrace, the birth
of our tiny, personal
and powerful nation—

now I mark a new era.

More Light

The cactuses want more light
than water. It continues to rain
outside where it can't reach them.
Chimes name the music
in the wind. And Beth's face,
pale in fluorescent plant light,
makes me want to live
my life. The curve of her back.
She's writing, and the glass tabletop
rings softly like a chalice.

Moonlight on Snow

The Vicodin night after surgery,
you floated to the bathroom, asked *Is*
that snow

or

moonlight? words like deer
stepping cautiously from the treeline.
Then back to bed and narcotic sleep.

Stranded, I watch for you.
Sand in my eyes. Tiny flakes
drift through spruce-green space.

The journey is long, waterways unknown.

You groan through drugs but do not rouse,
cannot pole your vessel any closer to me.
We've not seen the cut, the wound

of healing. I will watch over that too.

Humility

Newspapers, dried mud, grass
clippings, dog shit scraped
painstakingly from sole,
instep, and heel—
the welcome mat collects
the detritus of the world.

It sees this task as weakness.
No initiative.
No ambition.
Worst of all, no
backbone; everyone
knows what happens
to nice guys. Still, it receives

the astrologer and the one
who quotes the Bible
chapter and verse, the prof
who loves books
but not people so much,

a fireman who raises garlic,
the young woman
and her entirely legitimate son,
and the fisherman who also makes
electrical connections
all over the city.

All day and all through the night,
the doormat
gazes into the expanse of sky.

It contemplates the vast
and the circular
and is made humble.

Another Secret Letter (to my mother)

Through the living room's
clocked arch, and in the cushioned
privacy of the couch, I rebelled
against family dinner.

My third grade mind tested if my being
or my absence tipped any balance,
if I mattered in a large family
and an even larger world.

You touched the back of your hand
to my forehead, but I was sick only
in soul. Imagine that pathetic voice: *Nobody*
loves me. With the others

already around the long table,
you still took me
seriously, giving privileged
private time. What you said or did,

if anything, I don't know, but there was
beyond words a conviction: I, whatever
that upright pronoun means, am in-
valuable. From that evening on,

I recognized the passing breath
of love and tried to honor it. That certainty
got me off the couch to cross
boundaries of language

and class, of custom and faith
and find there
a whisper (*yes*), an affection
both familiar and involuted.

Everyday Shames: Pee-wee Football

Ok so there I was what
fourth or fifth grade
and Billy Darling
the coach's son wanted to play
defensive end   sick I guess
of being on the receiving end
of their work
and the first string quarterback
a guy I remember moving
like liquid in all the stutter
of pee-wee football   well he
had already moved away
leaving the pocket
empty   I saw my opening
and acted as quickly
as I could
I quit
makes it seem
easy when I was sick
not about my choice
but delivering the news
to my father
quitters we all know
never prosper never
get ahead   From the backseat
I told him   I hold a vision
of his eyes in the bright
rectangle of the rearview
He told how he
hated football   how his brother
would goad him
into playing one-
on-one and skewing the rules
ok you get
a twomississippi lead
and I pictured my father   a grown man
getting creamed
by my Uncle Don   a formidable
presence   My father
not only said

it was ok
that I quit but said *every person*
has unique gifts
gifts and talents
those eyes again
and maybe football
wasn't mine
but *you have something*
he said   *some gift to give*

A Favorite Memory Echoed in a Line from a Favorite Poem

Sundays in summer too my father
was irrepressible. Up early
and out of the quiet of the yellow house
to be on the tennis court while still cool,
he'd have a full day before I even woke.

We'd mill around the kitchen,
that cramped square kitchen, where someone
scanning the packed shelves of the open fridge
would complain there's nothing to eat.

Just then, he'd burst in—
Bunnie-bun-buns from Bunville!
as if in the time we were sleeping,
he'd invented his own language
or learned at Mass
how to speak in tongues. But by the grace
of sugar and flour, we understood
the love that emanated from him
like July heat.

We devoured the crullers
and powdered doughnuts, the rare
and coveted éclairs until the box
stood open and empty as the tomb.

A Blessing

for the birth of a niece

New one, perhaps
these words will fit you
like the booties
and overalls you will
certainly grow into and
out of. Soon enough
you will learn
how hard things
and people are. Remember
who you are and the voice
that is quiet within you,
that is great within us.
Your family, little one,
is nothing and all
there is. You belong
to all living things
first, and second
you are a human being.
So, practice compassion
to become skilled
in kindness. Then
your protection
will be your great
and many loves.
If I were there, I'd lean
to your tiny head,
kiss your fine
and delicate hair
to send you
with my blessing
into the world.

Twins

for the birth of a niece and nephew

Your parents were full of joy
—and weariness—when you were born,

and the people thronged the capital
straining our voices in a song against war.

You pushed into a world of lungs
and blood, where compassion and fear contend.

Washington in October is lovely
and delicate, a marbled city

where the Lincoln Memorial's white columns,
like cedar trees, soar away into azure skies.

Then, when you were offered to God,
water naming you with eternity,

we again poured into the streets
to say the redirecting word, to turn our nation

toward another future. Our leaders, nevertheless,
chose war. None of it can be taken back now,

not the protests nor the missiles.
I want to apologize to you, babies yet,

as you will grow to take your place
in history. Citizen-saints, you rely

on the power that saves us all: how much
and how often your mother puts herself aside

to feed you, first one then the other,
and soon the first again, and how often

your father walks you through dark rooms
and long halls until you sleep again

on his shoulder. Though tiny, you remind us
by your very being how to live,
as we all do, by the force of love.

Emptiness (The Middle Way)

When the clothespins
first heard the Buddha's
Middle Way—that instant—

they were convinced.
Not merely all-things-
in-moderation,

but the need for tension,
just enough to hold on
in sun and wind

and all the inner storms,
but not so much
to ruin the ride.

Like a crowd of disciples
they gather in the bag
enjoying the wooden

click of congregating
but they never lose
the joy of standing

alone on the line,
no shirt, no towel,
no weight, no purpose.

The Vow

You show me, Creekcurve,
    the loveliness of hillshapes
  in sunset light. That contrast,
that undulation we live in, we are.

Because aging is just another transformation

—bloodflow through cloudlungs,
geologic inhalations
become dewgleams
on autumn mornings—

I align my devotion in the passing:

I choose again today
    your scarred chest, I choose
you, your smile, your eyes:
body beauty is earth beauty.

Voluptuous

with its curves and neat dip
the spoon   guides what I need
to my mouth   it prides itself
on this rich service   makes itself
beautiful   in roundness

voluptuous   Rubinesque utensil
unique link between mineral
vegetable and animal
holding contradictions   in itself

of course it stirs and it ladles
even hangs like a pendulum
from some noses   the inner life
of the spoon is varied

but its heart belongs to the moment
of circular awe   when mouth
open and ready   joins spoon
and its cargo of hope

In a Cedar Tub

Nearly midnight
and traffic still goes on,
people not where
they want to be.

Up to my neck
in fire-warmed water,
my arms arc
the tub's round rim

and a school's lights
amber-stain the clouds.
We know by faith
stars burn above them.

Feet gripping the far wall,
I become a shallow cup,
an open parenthesis
in which you lie, half-

floating, half-stretching,
so our bodies declare
again a wordless fidelity.
Snow swirls around us

as we celebrate
our anniversary,
our union and reunion,
our lasting buoyancy.

from

HOUSE OF GREEN WATER

(FootHills Publishing, 2015)

Gorge

the power of a columbine
is its gentleness

the force of water
its yielding, the way

it lets itself
fall and flow

how it settles
how it reflects

and how it allows
finally allows

itself to go, disappearing,
rising, to begin again

the power of a gorge
is its openness

all that is not-there
shaping us

Self-Portrait, In the Eye of Stone

Glen Creek is a dammed torrent, a flood
slowed and tamed, though its current
twists and braids, and when its cords let go,
they are loosed as they are made
running chalky brown, the ground
ground down and flowing away.

See for yourself how time, too,
is sedimentary, trace the layers
in the watercourse of your own life.

Slate looks always upward
like a flounder or trilobite pressed flat
to the thickening ocean floor.

To be held in the eye of stone
is to know eternity, the build-up
and erosion of it. The child I was,

emptied himself out, worn away
grain by grain to become by degrees
the canyon of a man I am. From high overhead
and far upland, strands of water
still spill over the trail at Watkins Glen,
spraying off the smoothed rockface
to rainbow in the right light.

Spring Pond Song

Redwings came at the reeds
on the wing and from the side
to grasp them upright
and together ring the pond.

The water catches sun-slant
and sheen, the golden gleam
of later and later sunsets.
A circle of ripples opens its eyes.

Just above the surface,
the birds cling and call, sounding
life's far longing,
taking its measure.

At the Shelter

The metal roof makes a taut drum head
and the rain pounds it. Another inch an hour.
Cots in long rows. I lie on my back
not seeing the couple try to steal privacy,
not feeling the eerie red glow of the Exit signs,
not letting the hallways' fluorescents
bleed through my eyelids like they do,
and not hearing the gym doors' pneumatic sigh
every time they snap open and bang closed
every time a parent takes a kid to the bathroom,
that small, sleepy face blinking against the harsh light.

How can anyone sleep in here? And yet,
some do. And loudly. The sound of snarled indrawn air
tightens my guts. It's the same twisting
as when I picture the house and drowned yard.
Windows stare into brown swirl.
Or worse, windows are jagged holes
the water pours in. Couch and recliner
float awkwardly in the living room—blind boatmen
on tiny oceans. Then I tighten to remember
the pictures on the walls, albums in the cabinet.

I listen to the steady drumming of the rain,
the whole shelter brimming with the sound.
In my mind, I watch the atmospheric flow
part around us, gather in clouds, then fragment
into a million drops, each splintering
in a thousand splashes on roofs
but then it reassembles in gutters, along roads,
into creeks that fill and swell the swollen river.
All is releasing, all is gathering.

I open my eyes.
Still visible, the scoreboard's
just a dark outline in a darkening hall.
No one is winning
and we're running out of time.

At the Fire Station

I imagine the current pulling against the tires.
My body feels like a guy wire, singing
with the strain. I haven't eased,
I haven't let go, I haven't come back.

The radio's crackle sounded like rain
but Dad's voice sounded so calm.
He reported the truck had stalled
and the water was rising hard.

What can I trust
when movement stops?
How can I trust
when all that flows
becomes flat force?

Because one bridge had closed
I circled back to cross another.
I had seen all the black houses,
had seen the river topping the dike.

I kept all that out of my answer
and hoped it stayed out of my voice.
What I radioed to my father
swept away with the years.

"We're in trouble," he said
and wind blew across my heart.
"We're climbing up
onto the truck's roof."
That was his last message.

I remember all the little holes,
the microphone's million holes.
It was a grate with tiny openings.
I lowered my words into them

I tried to reach him,
but words are such small things,
It was 3 am
and all the lights were out.

What do I trust now
when darkness is all I know.
What can I trust
when silence contains so much?

It was 3 am and the lights were out,
so he plunged through the dark
and the river kept moving.
It is 3 am and I keep the lights out.

What can I trust when the past
never stops. It just keeps going.
What can I trust when the flow of it
is a blunt force pulling against me.

From Source to Mouth

We stand where rains
divide, some going north
to link lakes in a watery chain,
some flowing eastward and Bayward,
and others draining west
to the long river.

All is gathering,
all releasing
in the grand systole,
the great diastole.

Trace the word back
to its hidden spring,
the song
to its deep well:
find the source
and know the river.

Underground,
in darkness, under
roots and through soil,
in and around the plates
of rock that give, opening,
closing, yes—
there:
the creative
forces displacement.

And the spring's power
requires rain—the subterranean
depends on the terrestrial,
on storm fronts, on winds
which flow, as well, from high to low.

The sacred work
of creation
is liquid
and never ends.

Some rain sinks down,
disappears, or seems to,

but rises again
in all manner of green-shapes,
which we receive
to form our own darkness,
our own sources,
where the song begins.

Seneca

Before the lake
was a lake, a sea

of ice churned
its slow tides.

There are frequencies
beyond our hearing,

colors
we cannot see.

Below the lake
flows a saltvein,

a slow pulse
under the earth.

There are lifetimes
beyond ours:

there are lives
we live in,

a house
we are home in.

from
BACKYARD PASSAGES and GRACE STREET

(FootHills Publications, 2012, and Cayuga Lake Books, 2016)

the spirit is an endless process
of which we humbly partake

—Abraham Joshua Heschel

White on White

Sometimes this journey's
a snow-covered road, one
without traffic or streetlamp,

fat flakes diving at headlights.
All vanishing point, no focus,

white motion on white background.

*

Do you believe,
my brother asked,
*the Christmas card
creeds you sent?*
No response. I have

questions like letters
on the table, like notes
left in the rain. Today
is a shimmering
that falls across light.

I can't check
catechism boxes
but unwrap
the white figurines
of the Nativity,

stand them in the entranceway.

*

Fear-folded, my soul's cramped and sad.
Sin's the cause or so we're told—
so strong an exile it could almost be real.

On the altar I place this wordful consciousness,
this interposing phrase-finding:

the image of a wooden door, swinging
through its whole frame, threshold
and through passage, an image
out of division, imagined distance.

On which side do I stand?

A game is on Pascal insists,
          and heads or tails will turn up.
     What will you wager?

Thumb-rubbing such questions, worrying
a theological dream:
                    the house is burning,
flames burst through an upstairs window
making a tearing sound in the chest.

                    *

Under the stillness of the moon,
with snow covering names
on gravestones, around us

night's a witness to our frailty

and aspirations. As delicate
as owl flight is the wind.
Small glitterings all over the slate.

On the yarrow, a white heart.

Drought-Dry Heart

On the tan grass matted
    to pavement, a dark vein
rose up, its beetle-black eye

    shining. A grassblade,
one of few left green,
    rippled. For a heartbeat,

listening under the August sun, all held,
    all hovered. I couldn't see then
the tongue tasting the world's

    shape and texture,
but later, under the okra,
    his two copper stripes glowed

against the droughted earth
    and his salmon-pink tongue
was quick as a whisper.

    Then, time itself ripened,
fattening with all the ways a moment
    germinates long before:

before the snake eased out
    lawn-wise, before marigolds
dried to paper flames, before

    plants were set into moist soil,
before unbroken lawn was broken,
    this yard, this helixed instant, was on the rise.

             *

The heat bears down and wears out.
Digging a foundation six feet below:
soil like dust. Lightning snaps a cord
between earth and sky.
                 (Nothing new,
                      nothing added.)
The husk of the self desiccates
in the long drought between the knowing
and the doing.

                              (No longer waiting,
                    not yet wanting.)
Researchers in Colorado predicted hurricanes
would be wild animals. In the hills come morning,
fog outlines land-shapes: owl-head and humpback.

I want to recede into where words become flames
without air, eyes glittering in watery-dark,
summer's potato flowers, star circles through the night,
a jut of upright shale, a stone stalk in the lawn
just where I placed it. Take that long-considered action
and schooling around the ankles, here they come,
the doubts, all guppy-mouthed and nibbling.
                              (so it seems,
                    so it feels)
Love's the best first step,
     an answering gesture of rain
               soaking down
                         and soaking deep.

                              *

Oily skin. Hands
like vinegar.
Night's a moist tunnel
we crawl through
to reach summer's
constant oven.

Turtles, hoping
for soil damp enough
for eggs, cross
the highway;
sparrows flap
in the gray-white dust
of earth and pebbles.

In the fruit soup
chilled overnight,
bits of ginger
in smoothed
cantaloupe
look like thread-flecks
in paper

on which I write
my thirst for you.

*

bees bend the cornflowers'
thin stems   how blossoms spring back

a few drops on sunflowers
weigh down those prodigious heads

then rain

not the outrage against summer
we expected   more

slow revelation

of clouds darkening
of wind and delicacy

Chicory Flower Song

I face East Hill with the sun.
My shadow along the browned grass
stretches darkly between dying pines
along the highway, then crosses it
and then the hoops and stickers
along the far access road.

This other me diffuses
into all the nightshapes
that rise across wires
and up the useless rock
of the abandoned quarry.

*

Back inside where the piano is percussive
and stringed
I listen with several selves, remembering
the chicory's pale blue flowers.
Roadside common-sight, summer's everyday face,
no wonder I take no second look.
The chicory's little blossoms, surprisingly professorial,
imparted their findings after a season of research:

> *A matrix of aspiration,*
> *the self's*
> *a nest of small twigs, a breath*
> *inhaled by the world*
> *and slowly released, never separate,*
> *never alone, flowing through and flowing toward.*
> *Each instant's*
> *an act of creation.*
> *Light's fading imperceptibly*
> *and yet we perceive it.*

Phlox swayed along the musical creekbank,
a flim-flam of purple and white. A pair of goldfinches
swooped over Badger Creek to land on teasels,
stalks dry as a bamboo rake.

*

I lay my body down in a bed of cricketsong
and rise again to mist in the crowtrees.

The spirit's a vessel where light never bottoms,
where we pour in the glass beads
of our daily dreams, our countless endeavors,
each smaller than the last until talc-fine sand
fills in—though openings yet exist
where the undiscovered moves.

What I know slips a gap-toothed gear.
What I know of God couldn't illuminate
a cicada's wing. Still, I write these notes
to leave in the rain. I've been loved,

often extravagantly, and the wire of it
hums all the answer I seek. From the pulpit
with Om carved into its fragrant wood,
love's the only Gospel proclaimed.

Concelebratory, vibrations of being
fuse body and spirit, voice and will,
past and future
            word and silence and now
                this reading
                        our vast text.

                    *

The old quarry is filled again
with mist, so dense
there's a whole new hillside.

Distances creep up close.
The crickets keep their vigil.
End of August. Already
the air is crisp as fallen leaves.

Morning glories
understand darkness
well enough to bloom.

Backyard Passage

Pilgrims hope to walk off their homes
bowing to altars all along the way
until bow is altar and the way arrival.
Thomas Merton traveled to Asia
to learn *the highest of vows...*
There is no longer anything to be accomplished.
Nothing is vowed. No one vows it.
I too took off, packing a borrowed pickup for Ohio
then again for Japan where I was guest,
wide-eyed and appropriately lost.
To those passing through, I was host as well.
Now a wanderer in a narrow range,
I'm a householder who listens to crickets, to the moon's
high hum and its musical descent into dreams. I sleep deeply
in the warm glow of the body of my love.

*

I am trying to make it snow,
but late humidity curls the book's cover.
The year rolls over and crickets
burn the air. Summer still hangs
from the hummingbird's green throat.

The moon's gaining. Descending light
through afternoon clouds
creates corridors, lifelines fanning
across the entire valley. Blue-tipped,
the flames of grace flare up
beyond the personal.

Those whose scriptures burn within them,
whose icons and statues
are not objects to worship but fuel
setting the heart ablaze in compassion,
these are free to warm the traveler by love's hearth.

But where am I? Whom do I welcome?

In the backyard where one works out salvation
mowing and weeding this valley of tears,
                              (*so it seems, so it feels*

the gospel of diligence has been preached
as it has since creation's eighth day.
              patterns are pleasing

But cultivation's not nature wild
and harvest not all fallen apples,
windfall grace and lost world.
              and they make us eager)

Gaining, the moon's setting. On night's door,
the guest knocks and knocks
while sunset rounds the land
with its upsurging dream, tidal and arcing,
vermillion, aqua, orange. In this liveliness,

I take my pen again and fill a white landscape,
blue lines marking a narrow white yard.

                    *

Like the kitchen-quiet that gathers
around punched down dough rising again
in a ceramic bowl, or the silent
angle of owl flight between sassafras trunks;
like a cavern dripping limestone
from one lifetime to the next, where tourists
descend into the earth, small, awed;
like a hawk's cry in early evening
and the chill shivering through the blood—

          love takes elements
                  from each and all,
              transfiguring,
                      more verb than noun—

just like my neighbor who bent for hours
to grade his driveway against autumn's rough rain
with gravel and stones hauled from his own garden,
raking another layer finer than the one below—

faithfulness carries us into the cricket-womb.

                    *

In her great age by the sea,
Aunt Jane's lungs filled
with saltwater.

Step into moon-cold night,
breathe it. Grass and heather
all silvered. It's the mansion

of unknowing, mystery's home.
The spirit is process,
endless and inviting.

From the evergreen sky, distant
and near, an owl cry opens a hollow
that widens beyond the yard.

The passage into mystery always refreshes.
So receive my pledge, drooping spruces,
take my profession, grass of my heart:

I vow to vow nothing
I vow to be nothing
and to the passage be true.

In the company of night
and all its ambassadors,
the space shuttle returns to Earth.

What moves through leaves
a wake. In the wide V
of space, we attend to currents.

I am happy in our bed, your arm
across my chest, sleep and the moon
crossing us, slipping through.

                    *

The middle of November:
the asparagus, gone to fronds
(a fine gold-orange forest)
must come down.

Beth in her wool tam
is out digging the plots,
putting the garden to bed. She's cut

the fingertips off
another pair of gloves.
How drizzle draws
nobility around her.

Snow-Country Sojourn

The subject for today, down here, is the verb "to be,"
Snow falling, then sleet, then freezing rain.
                    —Charles Wright

Unanchored, my heart
leaf-drifts. Along the end-of-autumn
crickets sing the cool,
gray light of cloud-cast

as if no tumult were turning,
as if all were slow dawning.

I clip on my name tag
but don't know all I am.
Outside the window,
the trees barely ripple.

                    *

I'm a garage sale, remainder-minded.
I want to burn too,
                    shake off the shale self
layered in a waterdrone. Neighbors move away,
jobs get stuffed in drawers with the socks,
even the grateful faces, smiling now,
will age into TVs and dis-remembering.
What we do erodes,
                    who we are accretes.

                    *

The screensaver's all squiggles
in black background.

My eyes are delete keys.
I cannot be saved.

Outside, grass appears
beside snow.
Light stays after.

I feel desk-topped,
college-ruled. The pencil point's
down to the wood.

*

I used to stand at the window
overlooking rows and rows
of parked cars and feel my soul

follow sight to the line of trees.
Dark trunks. White snow. Straight
and leaning and fallen world.

Now I watch as side one, 36;
side one, 37; side one, 38.
The rhythm has calmness

and my mind goes as blank
as the copier's touchscreen.
And as small.

*

I want to shape my longing.
I want to want in certain ways.

Images tick-tick in the mind
like flakes of snow but none stick.

Is there logic to such passion?
I've grown stiff-armed and achy,

unaccustomed to this work.
I click off the light, savor the dark.

*

Rain-heavy grass dampens my shoes
—how quickly toes chill, how clear
the drops on black polish—

I think of the mountains of clouds,
upflow and change, the spirit moving;
I breathe out my molecules of desire
and join the long amplitude of life.

               no burning bush
            no great wellspring
               of gratitude

It takes effort,
I'm told, to crease

the mind's
habit in your direction.

                        *

I have been on my usual sojourn
into the cool territories
of tidiness and diligence.

I almost forgot your pulse,
my companion, your exuberance
and heart-heat, God-head.

This morning's birdsong marked your arrival
from the snow-country.

Your vastness, your vision, my bold self —

when pine needles and frost
gleam quick and go, I remember, I return

                        *

The dreaming life
                the golden eyes
of asparagus fronds that wave in slate wind

This life does not end
                does not go silent
like a casket room and dark clothes

So tell the story of green

need is the first book of seawash
and fern of green jewel
and eyes human

                        *

I have returned to find your voice
altered,
        slipped a register
like a knot that grips itself.

The lyrics of the hymnal
swim up
        dragging muddy tendrils.
All that bending.

And filling the air with wood chips.

I stop sawing—
                your insistent
                        movement
             and its easeful listening
                is the current I follow.

                        *

what is
is   :   being

explains itself   :   sunlight
powdering

frost in grass   :   all
essence

all transformation
(where death cannot hold)

                        *

A blue jay on the shoulder
muscles off into the trees.
The road's a ghost, flickering
black and gray after the snow season.
I live at a spirit address.

The Green Spiral

More blossoming here in your letter
than in the daily smudge of headlines.
Hello tenderness it says.

The old man
crumples slowly to the soil
where he will work

and work all day, thinking only
of return. The pain, he says,
worth it.

Just as a flock of greetings
was rising out of the trees
to head your way,

your words arrived
right when I needed them:
they say, *hello junco,*

and *isn't it delicious?*

                             *

What fuel for the fire? What hospitality?
The teaching is clear: its statements
are metaphors: neither if-driven nor sown
and tended by logic's fat thumb.

I am salt and you are salt.
I am light, you are light.
But flames die, room go cold.
So I say
         : beware of believing
            in only one figure

              : speech limits
                 as it illumines

       : draw close—embers even now
           ripple red and are lively

You are light, and you are more:
you are sage

long gone brittle
and you are the drying, the disintegration,
flow of fragrance
                    and blend of flavors,
          guest and host
               and the meal itself
          one seat empty for the wanderer

You are light and you are more
You are quartz
catching in tiny alcoves all the dark light

          :   write in the mysterious
                language of crystal

     love's the emptiness
     we seek, the oneness
     of no selves

                         *

In the black betweenness of space,
the unsubstanced
something defined by negatives
and the absence of familiars
                    there the door hangs,
                    plumb and neat:
ordinary wood, plain metal hinges,
sturdy frame boxing it out,
                              double-entry
servant door, yawning
open to one side then swinging open
the other. Unattached, unhoused,
a figure, so it seems, so it feels.

I breathe in, contracting atmospheres,
expanding others,
                    and the door moves
through its threshold, angling open
to allow in the vastness of time.

and I breathe out, releasing molecules
that dissolve into the process of creation
(*a part, not apart*)
               and back through its threshold

the door swings for all created radiance, angling open
to include all the vastness of material.

*

The ground is gray with dry.
Sweat builds on my neck,
at the small of my back.
Inside, the cats sleep and stretch
then sleep again. I fill the green
plastic watering can,
then when I tip it, sprinkling
the earth and seeds below,
the jug hums. Water pools
then disappears. Feverfew,
left in the fall and up early this year,
have been bursting with flower
for days. Like a fist
uncurling into an open hand,
a slow conciliation, this
awkward, devoted offering.

*

Green curls
    up through my life—
        in this spiral of mercy
    nothing's wasted
            nothing's held back.
    My walking is my answer.

*

Three monks in yellow
outside the conference
against the death penalty
chanted *namyo myoho*
renge kyo, tapping
hand-drums, the beat
under everything that lives.
I remembered your letter
wishing "spring flowers
fill your days ahead
and may time for poetry
and gardening abound for you."
Tulips, some still hiding

their secret faces
in the day's bloom,
of themselves opened, heating
with heartwarmth
the dew-cool grass
and maroon stigma tips
of the pear flowers.
Like the moment monks
sang the morning's
inherent holiness, time
fills and overflows,
a fountain, a seed
eastering always
in blossom-time.

from

10048

(Finishing Line Press, 2019)

From the beginning
the collapse of the World Trade Center
has been a tale told in numbers as well as words...
One number gets little attention,
but it should not be ignored in contemplating
Lower Manhattan's future. It is 10048.
That was the trade center's ZIP code.

—Clyde Haberman,
New York Times, November 14, 2003

The skyscraper as symbol refuses to die.

—Ada Louise Huxtable,
Wall Street Journal, September 17, 2001

Blowback

this goes into the bedrock of an island
and before the blueskies morning of September

an office building nine ten eleven stories high
could fit into the foundation hole the Ground Zero hole
the where-is-daddy hole the War on Terror hole

a hundred and forty six buildings
condemned and demolished to make room
what once stood is now gone for good
streets in lower Manhattan were blocked off
dug out and removed dump truck by dump truck
making real estate where once was only river

this goes way back and deep into the bedrock of a nation

                              *

"A group of mujahedeen
     who only a few years earlier
the US had armed

     with ground-to-air Stinger missiles,
grew bitter
     over American acts and policies

in the Gulf War....In 1993
     they bombed the World Trade center
and assassinated several CIA employees

     as they waited at a traffic light
in Langley, Virginia...."

                              *

It was metal, the mountain.
So much of the concrete
vaporized, crushed to particles.

As I ran north, I tasted
the World Trade Center on my lips.

from Gambits

in the time it takes to dial 911,
to order a cup of french roast, two sugars, extra cream,
to decide on the green or the blue blouse,
to log on and check the pileup of email,
in the amount of time it takes to breathe an Our Father,
to hail a cab and wait for it to pull up—
Our building swayed a long way
toward the Hudson River
to the west   And then it stopped
And then it came back to vertical
And then there was no back and forth
It didn't vibrate   It didn't oscillate
—you can see it frame-by-frame, watch it happening,
the ascending to vanishing, the blue, blue, the blue sky
and the tailfin all that's visible from the yet-smooth South Tower

                                *

Fake ID fit him
                          as a fake building contractor
and got him to the roof

but months of diagrams
                               got the crossbow
fit for flight. In Richard Nixon's

August of Shame,
                   Phillipe Petit, in a hard hat,
hauled all his gear

1000 feet up into the air,
                          his walking cable
assumed to be antenna equipment.

It took all night
                     to successfully arch the rope, pull
the cable, and ratchet it taut

so that at 7 am
                   as the first workers
were reaching the unfinished roof

he stepped into wind

              to kneel midway,
then, improbably,

lay down, spine
            to wire, face to sky,
and crowds to frenzy far below.

Seven crossings
            he walked (45 minutes)
to help "frame them in glory"

glory
     in what lies between,
in all that is absent.

Displacement

'The lines between *military* & *civilian*
    targets, between military & civilian
populations had been erased

during the aerial bombings of WWII.
    This is not what is new
since September 11.

The bombings of London by the Nazis
    & of Dresden,
Hiroshima, and Nagasaki by the Allies

dramatically crossed the line
    between military & civilian targets
in modern war.

[This is not what is new since September 11.]

The Algerian Resistance against the French
    aimed at destroying
the *normalcy of everyday life*

by blowing up French residents of Algiers
    in cafés, markets, & train stations,
reminding them not only

they were the enemy
    but there could be no "normal life"
[What is new since September 11?]
                    *

Taped to mailboxes, curved around lamp posts,
slapped up on any flat wall or window,
even on cars parked long enough,

the faces, the lost faces, disappeared
and longed for, the faces stared out at the as-yet-
still-live ones who passed the passing.

Remember how candles pooled and flickered
under flowers that laced chain link
and how on the fence was a photograph:

a white-veiled woman enwrapped

by her tuxedoed groom, and you couldn't
you couldn't tell who was missing and who

who was yearning, so you'd read the name
and learn she worked for Cantnor
up on the 90-something floor. Maybe the husband

and their two little girls photocopied
these sheets and, stapler and tape in hand,
walked street after street, glad

at least to be active in that awful waiting,
knowing and not wanting to know.
This was in the days we lined up for hours

to donate blood, remember? Blood
that was never needed. Of course
you don't. —We're ghosts talking to ghosts.

Before they footnote it, Cantor Fitzgerald,
a bond-trading firm, lost 700 out of 1000 employees.
Its offices occupied floors 101

through 105 of the North Tower,
the one struck first by American
Flight 11 at 8:46 am.

Poetry pours out through the net
of explanation. Have you seen
Amy O'Doherty? Adriane Scibotta?

Chris Kirby, 152lbs, blue eyes, a carpenter...
Tonyell McDay, ruby ring on left pinky finger...
Colleen Supinski, large blue eyes...

Francis (goes by Frank or Fran)—
two tattoos: one a Shamrock
in Irish flag colors over "Mom"

in the middle of his left arm,
and on his right
the kanji for "Mother."

from Descent

I was standing in front of the hotel. I'm a doorman
          I was in line at Starbucks
          I was in Ms. McKenna's third grade class
          I was at Mass
          I was sleeping when the phone rang

Is the point that tips forward
into a new era where we stood so that

                    time
                    becomes

location, a footprint on earth,
a place once functional, once measurable
square footage tallied as real estate as

                    intersection
                    becomes

symbol

          8:46 —› 10:29
          9:03 —› 9:50
              10 : 03

          I was waiting a table
          at a restaurant in Soho
          and I literally saw a
          it seemed to be a
          small plane it looked like it
          bounced off the building
          and then
          I just saw a huge ball of fire on top of the building...

When did you realize it was deliberate?

How many hours of TV did you watch?

Who did you know and why were they there?

For how many days did you sleepwalk?

Who saved your life, who pressed your body
to theirs, who held you in that balance?

*

*"Maybe the walls of Jericho fell down
because they weren't built on good foundations."
—John Kyle, Chief Engineer at the Port Authority*

The shelf runs south, and as it runs
it sinks farther and farther under Lower Manhattan,
and the bedrock stretches under Staten Island
and through New Jersey. This is the foundation
of the foundation, like liberty under laws.

For the World Trade Center, they had to dig out
all the layers of accumulated landfill—
old bricks and rubble, hand-forged nails,
a century-old slipper, cannonballs
and a cannon muzzle, several clay pipes,
ancient anchors, including a 1000-pound hulk
it took nineteen men to haul out—
the leavings of Colonial, Federal, and all our other
previous versions, our neighbors in time,

then they dug out the oozy black mud,
river silt, Hudson River silt, sediment
once suspended in currents and tides
that settled out and layered down
to coat docks and whole sunken ships,

then came bull's liver, yards and yards
of the stuff—maybe another story's worth—
red sand that fills in as you dig it out,
like a beach hole that gets wider
but only slowly goes deeper,

next comes clay, hardpan
packed by glaciers and their boulders,
now we're time traveling, 10,000 years,

and finally,
below the hardpan and quicksand of bull's liver,
and under the oddments of garbage till,
finally, the backbone of the island:
where there is no under, no further back,
where the country is no more,
where we are still the land's
before the land is ours.

from Imagination, And Its Limits

It was heat, not impact.
Melting, not velocity.
Fuel, not force. Then,
mass rode gravity.

Engineers imagined airliners,
of course; the towers
were designed to absorb
and withstand concussions

but imagining couldn't account
for capacity, in passengers
and so in fuel, for the scale
of 21st century (barely)

aircraft. Imagination
begins somewhere; its limits
are hidden until, like glass,
they're breached.

From his office just streets away,
structural engineer, Les
Robertson witnessed
his creation's fate *Yes,* he says,

*we watched it, and you could
reach out—*
his hand goes to the window
and the gap

in the skyline
*—and touch it.
But there was nothing
you could do.*

*

February 26, 1993.
Because we didn't notice,
didn't heed, they didn't stop:
Six dead.

Rented vans. Urea Nitrate,
a source of fertilizer, to feed

crops. Or fuel poison.
The theory: one tower

tripped from underground
(bomb in the parking garage)
would topple the other.
But the van wasn't packed

to its one-ton capacity;
the fire consumed
the sodium cyanide.
My greatest regret,

said Ramzi Ahmed Yousef,
was not using
enough explosive.
Only six dead.

Sound Waves

Do you remember the stillness
    (despite the always-on
    I-can't-take-it-anymore
    buildings-coming-down news)
the empty skies—
four days
no flights.

Schools closed. Football games canceled.
Hollywood stopped filming, the Emmy's postponed.
Internet sites crashed.

From a NYC police copter
one witness reported:
    a vast cloud of smoke, dust
    and debris engulfed
    the financial district.

    Buildings disappeared
        boats fled the scene.

    There was silence.

    In the helicopter
    —the collapse, the cloud
    made no sound,

    and no one spoke.

            *

Harry Druding
raised the four foot rebar
—equipment shut off
so all could listen
to the stone's voice.

As much as sixty feet
below street level, workmen
struck bedrock, then blasted
to reach steadier stuff.
When solid layers
revealed themselves,
they chiseled.

Now they were poised.
Waiting. Motionless.
Gaps and faults
would register
in muffing tones:

Druding swung
and the metal made
a sweet ping

on which all the concrete,
all the steel, aluminum,
and each of the 43,600 windows
would rest. Listen:

                    *

Overhead, a roaring,
and it got closer and closer.

In the walls, in the skewed building—
a grinding, a squealing,
something I never heard
even in the worst storm.

When the tower righted itself
there was a bubble—no fire alarm,
no announcement on the intercom. Nothing.
Just that bubble of quiet.
Which was worse.

I heard one of the firefighters mumble,
"We've got jumpers."

Every half a minute, oh God,
the bodies never stopped.
Every thirty seconds
the horrible crushing sound
echoed through the lobby.

It was a freight train,
the sound twisting steel makes
straining to hold
against the stress within it.

The undercover cop was muttering,

"This thing could go, this thing
could go, this thing could go."

Sirens. Coming from everywhere.
Vanishing in the distance.

The sound of no dial tone.
Every pay phone I tried.

Hacking. Everyone coughing
through handkerchiefs and shirtsleeves,
coughing their lungs out.

"You believe this? No way
am I ready for this."
Then the sergeant shouted, "Go, go, go!"

The faraway sound, like someone
was trying to reach me,
but it was me, saying *I gotta
get out of here. I gotta find my wife.*

Weeks later, the CEO's voice over
the airline company's intercom
asking for a moment of silence.

The Tallest Building in the World

In America, ambition fueled
moon-flight. What is it

about breaking the four minute mile
or scoring a 100 points in a game?

In the flea circus, the matchbook
is the tallest building in the world.

In the land of plenty, the home
of winning-isn't-a-sometime-thing,

a cut-throat culture stretches from Green Bay
to Pelican Bay, from Annapolis to Guantanamo,

from sea to purple mountain majesty.
So you'd think that when Minoru Yamasaki

agreed to design the World Trade Center,
everyone set out for the highest building ever.

But that came later. First, he strove
to 'scale it to the human being

so that it will be inviting, friendly
and humane.'

'Warmth and human scale.'
Standards of the spirit.

What measures transcendence,
the depth of wisdom, or love's

tensile strength? These are never listed
in the *Guinness Book of World Records.*

This land and its people abide
and embody—*Do I contradict myself?*

Very well then.—these contradictions,
their material and intangibility,

in our grief for towers now gone
and in wars that grind on.

*

"the chain of events from the US
    arming and training of Afghan
and Al Qaeda mujahedeen

    to fight the Soviets in Afghanistan
to the Taliban and Al Qaeda
    and its international network

including fighters sent to
    Bosnia-Herzegovina
    Somalia
    Chechnya
    Central Asia
is direct."

*

There were 40,000 doors
in the World Trade Center buildings

Each door is a frame
        each frame a cut

    each cut a hand
each hand a story

And like molten steel or liquid glass
into that hole America poured story after story

from Corrugated

Dear friends, denied seats on the same flight,
said their goodbyes at Boston's airport, then boarded:

one on American, the other on United.
American, United. Untied later, Americans

taped flags to brick walls, attached them
to car windows, tied them to fences on overpasses.

The Stars and Stripes forever. Notes posted
above flowers, photos, more Old Glories—*Remember not*

the horrors, one sign read, *only the heroism.*
These were prayers, physical psalms rising to heaven

from dusty questions: Can we know humanity
without knowing grief? The word *al Qaeda*

means *the base* or *foundation,* but there's something
deeper down, isn't there? When does night end

and day begin? Their mantra was 'the necessary
permits the forbidden.' Our refrain was a slogan

I misremember as *These colors do not bleed,*
so the flag's red stands stark in my mind against sky blue.

The stars' bright blaze asks, Can we mourn
and seek revenge simultaneously?

We do it all the time. Those aren't the poles that oppose.
Grief fuels rage, the desire to destroy and make bleed.

Can we seek revenge and make justice? Morning was still dark
as passengers streamed toward Logan. Ruth Clifford McCort

and her daughter, Virginia, were headed to LA.
So was Ruth's best friend, Paige Mackel. Is our answer

our mourning? Something deeper, there must be
a foundation below the foundation, emptiness

folded within matter where all that's still possible moves,
where re-arrangements happen by happy chance,

where no future is fixed and no feeling final.
Ruth and her daughter boarded United Flight 175

which crashed into the South Tower. Ruth's brother,
Ronnie, dashed into the intersections that grid

Lower Manhattan, and phoned Ireland. Their brother there
worried about Ronnie's trip to New York,

neither of them aware of the fate of those above him.
Time corrugates to make space for unknowing,

for unlearning what seems obvious, like the difference
between friend and enemy, the living and the dead,

the solid and the fluid, the past and the passing.
Mohammed Atta's second piece of luggage from Portland

didn't make it, and so officials found the handbook
which says, "Angels are calling your name."

That bag circled the carousel for hours. That's one ending
to the story. The other stays with the question

until the rabbi says night will not end
until our vision is keen enough

to look on the features of any man or any woman
and recognize a brother, a sister.

                              *

No photos, buddy, the officer commanded,
punching him in the shoulder,
This is a crime scene. Even so,
movie lights illuminated
the whole night scene:

amid the metal wreckage
of I-beams and twisted columns,
an odd collection of plastic cafeteria
and leather conference chairs,
there was an enormous book:

as many as ten stories of the building
were compressed into the space of about a foot.
Ignoring the cop's directive,

the photographer obeyed
the eternal command: *Take and read.*
He wandered all over the Pile
where the Bathtub's exposed wall
loomed again and the river
seeped through. Picture the fireman,
whose shift had ended but who couldn't leave:

"We're gardeners," he said still working his rake,
"in the gardens of the dead."

from Gravity

It was Italians and Italian-speaking
Americans who engineered and drilled down through
fill, silt, and sand to slam into bedrock,
where they could find it.

After laboring 14-hour days, George Tamaro,
Jersey native, with a little one
on the way, routinely got roused
by phone calls. In this sleepless way,
he moved The Bathtub along.
Not a tub to soak in, this one
kept water out, sealing foundations
against the Hudson. A wall to encircle
eleven of the westernmost acres.

Digging for a panel along Greenwich
(a part of which itself would float away,
sink in the river, and become
Battery Park City),
drilling didn't stop, all that air
where schist should be—

the underground cave
and neighboring hundred-foot valley
was hollowed by glacial streams
and the power of gravity—
though the watercourse was gone,
though the ice sheets were gone.

We understand now what they couldn't then:
our dearest companion is the missing.

*

The falling man, the man on wire,
the vertical tension of the scale
and the physical tenderness
of the body, the individual life,

the individual man, falling
but in the photo hanging as if from a wire,
gravity's relentless, inevitable tension suspended;
the result: an odd tenderness

for the elegance of the image
and its gravity, as it hangs
in memory as if on a gallery wall,
the Towers' vertical body

framed in memory and in such artifacts,
their scale increasing as grave
as symbol, and yet there is more:
there is this individual feeling,

a feeling in the body, a tenderness
for another human being, a person—
and for a moment we remember
the elegant body of our kinship.

from Domino Theory

'They came from the Kingdom
   that houses and protects
the holy places of Islam

   and it is at the same time
a filling station
   for the Western economy.

(source of one fifth of America's petroleum)

The goal was first
   clear Saudi Arabia
and its oil fields

   of American personnel
then, take over Pakistan
   and its atomic arsenal.

Acts of religious terror
   are not done for the sake
of farmers, workers,

   students
or oppressed
   and helpless people.

They are done
   in the name of God.
But God will not reply to them.'

Freefall

Down flight after flight,
she finally reached the lobby.
Sprinklers soaked her.
But then: behind
and beyond her:
a strange rumble:
nearly a third of a mile
of glass and metal:
the whole South Tower
collapsing.
Second struck, first to fall.
So this is it, she thought,
this is the end. After walking
down all those stairs.
But then: a policeman
grabbed her, hauled her
downward again,
into the subway, the shuddering
crush all around now, down
as if into their own grave.

*

I thought I was blind. The air blast
like a hurricane stormed through the concourse
and blew me to my knees, into water
and broken glass. When I opened my eyes:
I can't see anything anymore,
I heard my colleague call out.
Dust blackened the air.

*

Cotton balls. It felt like
being stuffed with black cotton balls.

*

Now that it wasn't a rescue mission,
all through the North Tower, the same command:
"Get out! Get out!" Firefighters dropped gear,
reversed direction. Below the 96th floor
the building was evacuated.

"Clear out. Down now." Down,
winding around those same stairwells
they'd just mounted. At the 16th,
debris stopped them, debris
from the other building, from
the destroyed, "Stairwell B—let's move,
come on, let's move!"

At each level, open the door,
point bullhorn, shout, "Get out,"
The same ritual, into emptiness.
Until the 12th floor. There,
50 - 70 people sat in an office.
He couldn't believe his eyes.
What were they thinking?

Only then did he make out
the crutches and wheelchairs.

                    *

The morning started out
hoping for the kind of day
you could repair lawnmowers
at the stationhouse.

                    *

Tons, hundreds of tons reached
freefall speed, the velocity of a body,
tie pointing skyward
when the North Tower imploded.
And in the lobby, crushed girder
and twisted-but-intact beams
created a hollow, a cave
in the mountain of metal
where a handful of survivors
coughed, eyes stinging,
voices thinned by the strain—
alive, they were alive
in a chamber made of chance.

The survivors found themselves
before anyone else found them
in a stairway jutting from the rubble,

a capsule launched somehow
to the edge of ruins.
Everyone there was rescued.

*

The bodies on the ground
were not always motionless.

Diligence

To pilot a commercial airliner,
one needs to be part of a team
and work together well.

One must be dependable,
self-disciplined, a role model.
"Can the candidate take criticism?"

The owner of Florida
Flight Training called one terrorist
"the perfect candidate"—

helpful to others,
cheering up classmates
when they got down. They liked

having photos taken
with him. He was punctual,
always in a good mood.

*

The money came in small amounts.
Into separate accounts
from separate points of origin.
No regular pattern. Perfect.

You can't get far down these streets
not-made-of-gold before *smack!*
running headlong and wallet-wise
into a bank. Go to Maine's
Acadia and listen
to the gravel crunch of Rockefeller's
carriage roads. Head to the Adirondacks
and walk through the Great Camps;
those rustic estates, which had electricity
before the surrounding towns,
were built for and staffed year-round
for the get-away of America's
captains of industry.

The money came in. Money
to rent an Altima

idling outside the Comfort Inn,
to pick up dinner at Pizza Hut,
to hold the apartment in San Diego
where the logistics team
slept on bare mattresses
and owned no other furniture,
through they carried briefcases
and took cell phone calls
as they ducked on occasion
into the limousine that came for them,
like bankers—strange, strange bankers.

And the money still came in. Money
to take a room at an EconoLodge
or disappear into well-off anonymity
behind the community's gated front,
to grab a copy of Microsoft's
Flight Simulator '98
or buy more Marlboro Lights for Atta
or purchase two first class
United tickets for $4,500

or tip the dancer
at the Olympia Garden Topless Club.

A young teller, counting wire transfers,
tallies them for account #5730000 259 772,
a most unpoetic detail. The poetry
is in her diligence, the banality
of virtue.

*

Siad Jared learned to fly,
passed his pilot's test
without difficulty, but his other mission
for more than a year was to live
amid the enemy, cheerfully accept
instructions from him. He was to
get to know his enemy, party
with him, laugh with him
—and at the end
still be able to kill [him.]

Not the window washer
who'd left home in Jersey at 5am
to be at his glass on time;
not the Cantor secretary;
not Albero Dominquez, a passenger
from Sydney, Australia, father of four;

not any particular person, not the enemy
as an individual, only as narrative,
an abstraction
no number of dead
can make real.

from Echoes

Mornings, elevator doors split open
    Salaam Aleichem
    Peace be upon you
a construction worker might greet
an electrician, but the chorus back
    Aleichem salaam
came from the suits too.

Financial execs, investment
   bankers, insurance brokers

      from Jakarta and Abu Dabbi,
      Dubai and Manchester,

   all in New York
for the rituals of business

and all passed through those elevators
to join the enterprise
of shrinking the globe through trade.
And so achieve peace.

Many found their way to the Prayer Room
on the 17th floor of the South Tower,
a room set aside for a different ritual:

first in a small washroom
   to cleanse hands, face, and feet

  and then to face east
and intone the *salat* prayer

The Afghan Trap

Take a small domed cage
suspended from a tiny pulley,
drop a silver ball down a long,
grooved slope, dinging a bell
along the way, and watch it
speed up for the jump,

so that for an instant, the metal sphere
doesn't touch any part
of the Goldberg contraption—will it sail
the gap? will it trip the lock
and drop the newfangled mousetrap?
will the unwitting prey wait that long?

These and other questions
hung in the calculating air, 1979,
as the Carter Administration constructed
The Afghan Trap, though we were after
far larger game than some pesky rodent:
we wanted to catch the lumbering bear

of the Soviet Union. No one wants
to poke directly at a baited bear,
so the Afghan Trap consisted of this:
gather and train Islamic fundamentalists
in Pakistan, then unleash them
on the communist puppet running Afghanistan

not to overthrow the government
(we now call such machinations
"regime change") but agitate and
destabilize, antagonize
just enough—that's the delicate part—
just enough to draw the Soviets

into their own debilitating Vietnam.
Like cartoon mice loosed in the circus
cause elephants to stand upright
on their yellow and blue risers, shrieking
and pulling up their costume skirts—
this was a gambit without regrets.

When questioned, in fact, in 1998,
former National Security Adviser
Zbigniew Brzesinski posed his own follow-up:
What is more important to the history
of the world? The Taliban
or the collapse of the Soviet Union?
Some stirred up Muslims or...

But why choose? A remarkable machine like this
could do both and still make it rain marshmallows.
Regret what? he asked. *Why all these questions.*
Lift the tiny cage and the crowd gasped
at the rubble stones of the Bamiyan Buddhas
and Fritz Koenig's gashed metal *Sphere.*

*

"Anything can happen
   when human beings allow
ideology to trump

   their humanity, when they elevate
an idea
   above the lives of individuals.

Anything
   can happen, and too often
does."

*

"Did Mohammed Atta
smell of fruity Comfort Inn Botanical Shampoo"
in the dark of morning
after showering in his non-smoking room
in Portland, Maine? We don't know.
But he was sure to follow the manual's instructions
to "not leave your house
unless you are washed and clean,
for the angels will forgive you
if you are clean." We do know
he left his house. That much, we know. That
and when they checked in,
they paid in full—$149.
They had an early flight,
so they'd be up and out.
Such strange courtesy.

What to do with such gestures?
How do we account for the fact
that one of the Strongmen,
whose task on the plane is clear
from his title, took in his hand
the motel keeper's hand,
thanked her, and said, "It was good
knowing you. You are a very good person."

Project Safe Flight

Before the site was a foundation hole,
but after it was a construction site,
two residents did not wish to leave:

One gazed from his penthouse window
atop a five-story office building
at his beloved river views.

The other, who had escaped
the about-to-be-demolished pet shop,
holed up in a beam-nest, raiding
area fruit stands to survive. The monkey
managed to elude workmen for months.

                    *

"After September 12
     no one was found alive
and the dogs

     were distressed.
It became necessary
     to stage situations

where 'survivors'
     were found by the dogs
to keep up their morale."

                    *

Following hour after exhausting hour,
they turned in flight, circling,
confused by lights not in the sky
but somehow in the sky nonetheless.
Drawn from millennial flyways, drawn
and disoriented, migrating birds
orbited two great hazards: light
and glass. Eventually,
some of these air travelers
descended into the city to land
and rest in trees and shrubs in planters.
Come dawn and the rising of the sun,
in the World Trade Center's vast plaza,
they were trapped in a maze
of invisible walls and reflected shapes.

Birds battered against the same windows.
At the base of the towers, volunteers
recovered hundreds of bodies.

The project, then, was simple: webcams
trained on the long vertical walls revealed
which floors remained illuminated (and so
attractive) and which windows
proved most dangerous. Tenants
were eager to help and the Port Authority
netted the insides of the glass.
In this way, the death toll was diminished.

Years later, after the towers were gone,
beams of light towered into the now-
disorienting space, and inside these bright shafts
white specks glittered. *It was hard,*
one witness said, *not to think of souls.*
In the dark of the moon, flocks
followed the guidance of starlight,
but were bedazzled and caught up
in the brilliant memorial.

American Redstarts, Baltimore Orioles,
thrushes and warblers were released,
freed from their circling flight
when the lights were shut off.
Just twenty minutes, but a gift,
a dark gift for other lives, still on the wing.

Preserving the Fabric

The snap of the tablecloth
echoed down the stairwell
of the North Tower. Can a sound
sanctify? Do prayers rise or float
or make anything happen?

Between 106 and 107, on a landing,
they laid out a small white field
—one of them flattened the last
olive oil box for a mat—
and made a space for devotion,
an island of spiritual devotion
in the great sea of capitalism.

Muslims from the Ivory Coast,
Morocco, Malaysia—immigrants
and citizens and visitors—
a most American mixture.

Between one floor and another,
between daylight and full night,
between earth and sky,

they gathered, and there
they prayed and together
they broke their fast.

                    *

"History
      is always
political. It never

      rips in two.
The discontinuities
      of the past

always
      remain
in the whole cloth."

                    *

The roaring reaches us

before we reach the place where
some say "their souls
are crying"
           where absence is preserved,
where water pours into squares
and there falls into smaller chambers.

It's not silence but a private veil
of sound, a watery drape
that makes of cityspace a stillness,
one we can inhabit
                if only a moment,
a bead of time to finger lightly.
We inhabit but cannot stay
for we are travelers
who have not yet arrived.

Long after we return to Omaha
or Tokyo, Tallahassee or Seattle,
London, Cincinnati, Istanbul, or Mumbai,
the water will go on falling
and falling
will tell the story of falling.

Notes

My books often include additional notes on references, but *10048* relies on the work of so many others that I want to acknowledge the following sources:

"Blowback"

—"a group of mujahedeen" from Chalmers Johnson's *Blowback: The Cost and Consequences of American Empire.*

—"As I ran north..." by Christine Haughney in "The Flow of Humanity" in *At Ground Zero: 25 Stories of Young Reporters Who Were There.* NY: Thunder's Mouth Press, 2002.

"Gambits"

—Petit section: from *Smithsonian Nov 2001*, "Turning Point" by Robert Chelminski. There's also a documentary film, *Man on Wire*, that depicts Petit's project, and in the novel *Let the Great World Spin*, Colum McCann writes an exquisite scene of him practicing in a field. I never found a way to integrate Petit's phrase, "When I see oranges, I juggle" into these poems though that kind of compulsion animates many aspects of this enterprise.

— Zeckendorf + D. Rockefeller section based on material in *City in the Sky: The Rise and Fall of the World Trade Towers* by James Glanz and Eric Lipton. NY: Henry Holt, 2003.

—"our building swayed" from Brian Clark's "Accounts from the South Tower" *NYTimes* May 26th, 2002.

"Displacement"

—"The line between military..." is from Seyla Benhabib's essay "Unholy Wars, Reclaiming Democratic Virtues" in *Understanding September11.*

"Descent"

—"I was standing...doorman." was spoken by Wendell Clyne, "I was waiting a table..." Stuart Nurick in *What We Saw by CBS News,* Simon & Schuster, 2002 recounts the phone interviews with Bryant Gumbal just 4 minutes after the first plane struck.

"Sound Waves"

—Harry Druding is profiled in Glanz + Lipton's *City in the Sky*

—The copter report is from *Above Hallowed Ground: A Photographic Record of September 11, 2001 by the Photographers of the NYC Police Dept.*

—Some sounds are recorded in various accounts in *What We Saw by CBS News.*

"Corrugated"

—The photographer in the gardens of the dead is Joel Meyerowitz, who gained access to Ground Zero and took pictures for 9 months. Sarah Boxer profiled his work in "Even in the Moonscape of Tragedy, Beauty is in the Eye." *NYTimes,* May 23, 2002

"The Tallest Building in the World"

— Yamasaki quote in Glanz + Lipton's *City in the Sky*

—"the chain..." from Susan L. Woodward "On War and Peace-Building: Unfinished Legacy of the 1990s." *Understanding September 11.* NY: The New Press, 2002. 212-237.

"Gravity"

—George Tamano from Glanz + Lipton *City in the Sky*

—*The Falling Man* is the title of a photo by Richard Drew. The profound documentary of the same title explores the experience of those who jumped.

"Diligence"

—Detail on the perpetrators from *Inside 9/11.*

"Project Safe Flight"

—The pet shop escapee monkey peeks through Glanz + Lipton's *City in the Sky.*

— "After September 12" about the rescue dogs from *Above Hallowed Ground.*

—Details about the birds from NYC Audubon Society ("It was hard not to think of souls.") and information about safeguarding birds is from a press release by the Port Authority of New York and New Jersey entitled "Port Authority Takes Steps to Protect Migratory Birds around World Trade Center." September 8, 2000.

—Brendan Keim. "9/11 Memorial Lights Trap Thousands of Birds." September 14, 2010. *Wired Science.* wired.com.

"Preserving the Fabric"

—The image of praying in the stairwell comes from a detail in Samuel G. Freeman's *New York Times* article "Muslims and Islam Were Part of the Twin Towers' Life" published on 10 September 2010. He says most were employees at Windows on the World who didn't have time to get to the mosque four blocks away.

—"History / is always / political" from Joanne Meyerowitz "History and September 11: An introduction" from the special September 2002 issue of *The Journal of American History.*

—Images of the water falling honor Michael Arad's design for the World Trade Center memorial, which he calls "Reflecting Absence" and which is profiled in Martin Filler's "A Masterpiece at Ground Zero" in the New York Review of Books 27 October 2011. When I wrote this section, I had not yet visited this memorial in person.

Acknowledgments

Much gratitude goes out to the editors of the following publications where my poems originally appeared, sometimes in slightly altered form:

2 Bridges Review: "Gravity"

Abiko Quarterly: "Pilgrimage to a Gingko Tree" (Editor's Choice) and "Delta" (Honorable Mention, 1994)

America: "In a Cedar Tub" (awarded third place)

Amoskaeag: "you do the math"

Barnabe Mountain Review: "Guest"

Between the Lines: "Displacement"

Blast Furnace: "The Display Models"

Brain of Forgetting (Ireland): first section of "Blowback" as "Going Back, Going Under"

Christian Science Monitor: "Voluptuous"

Common Ground: one section of "Backyard Passage"

Ekphrasis: "The Bridge"

Extracts: "Twins, "Another Secret Letter," and "Emptiness (The Middle Way)"

Fathoms: "First Frost"

Festival: "Grace Street"

Fresh Ground: two sections of "The Green Spiral" ("What fuel for the fire?" nominated for a Pushcart Prize)

Hiroshima Signpost: "Sandankyo (I)"

International Quarterly (Fifty Years of Fallout Issue): "Aioi" and "Delta"

Japan Environmental Monitor: "Gingko"

Japanophile: "Another Journey"

Loyalhanna Review: "Stuart Little, Yellow House, Avalon, NJ"

Mississippi Valley Review: "The Missing"

Mud Season Review: "Preserving the Fabric"

parting gifts: "The Romantic Quest," "Guest," "How Ants Felled Two Trees," "In the Shadow of Shirakiyama," and "Everyday Shames: Pee-wee Football"

Poetry East: "Into Darkness"

Red Jacket: "Pilgrimage to a Gingko Tree"

Rock & Sling: "Chicory Flower Song"

Sightings: "Passing"

Sojourners: "All Burning"

Spiral: "Walking Meditation"

Temenos: 2 sections of "(With Roethke) in a Watery Drowse" ("I've been reading..." and "My father worked...") in a special Roethke tribute edition

The Cape Rock: "The History of Love"

The Kerf: "The Vow" (nominated for a Pushcart Prize)

The Misfit: "The Discontent of Everyday Objects"
The Other Side: "Origami," "The Night Cafe," "Crossing Motoyasu Bridge,"
    and "Cosmos"
The Other Side: "Like Superman,"
The Penwood Review: "White on White"
The Whirlwind Review: "Project Safe Flight"
Third Wednesday Journal: "Moonlight on Snow"
Three-Lobed Burning Eye: "Passing Bell" and "Times Like These"
US Catholic: "To One Born in a Time of Crisis"
West Branch: "Why I Think About Hiroshima & Nagasaki"
Wind Magazine: "R5: The Paoli Local"

The anthology *Atomic Ghost: Poets Respond to the Nuclear Age* included the poem
"Why I Think About Hiroshima & Nagasaki."

The anthology *Come Together: Imagine Peace* included the final section of
"The Green Spiral."

Paul Quayle's photo book *Hiroshima Calling* included "Origami."

Special thanks to Michael Czarnecki, small-press publisher, poet, and Chinese
sage living in the hills of upstate New York. He published my first freestanding
chapbook as well as two others. Because of Michael's dedication to providing
poetry whenever possible, *House of Green Water* appeared the same week as the
concert that featured those poems as lyrics, a collaboration with composer Will
Wickham called *Where Sacred Waters Divide.* I'm grateful for Michael's devotion
to poetry, and his artful care in making lovely books.

This work of thirty years bears only one name on the cover, but I am deeply
indebted to many whose influence and support contributed, particularly John
Bradley, Ken Letko, Mike Aquilina, Scott Minar, Margaret Kasper Reed, Mary
Hood, Bonnie Warden, Margaret Gibson, and John Balaban. I would not be the
poet (or person) that I am were it not for two women in my life: Kate, my cousin,
mentor and anam cara, and Beth, the love of my life, best friend, and mutual
helpmate, ever. Gratitude wells up in me when I consider these benefactors.

About FutureCycle Press

FutureCycle Press is dedicated to publishing lasting English-language poetry in both print-on-demand and Kindle formats. Founded in 2007 by long-time independent editor/publishers and partners Diane Kistner and Robert S. King, the press was incorporated as a nonprofit in 2012. A number of our editors are distinguished poets and writers in their own right, and we have been actively involved in the small press movement going back to the early seventies.

Each year, we have awarded the FutureCycle Poetry Book Prize and honorarium for the best original full-length volume of poetry by a single author that we published that year; if no original collections are published, no prize is offered. Introduced in 2013, proceeds from our Good Works projects are donated to charity. Our Selected Poems series highlights contemporary poets with a substantial body of work to their credit; with this series we strive to resurrect work that has had limited distribution and is now out of print.

We are dedicated to giving all of the authors we publish the care their work deserves, offering a catalog of the most diverse and distinguished work possible, and paying forward any earnings to fund more great books. All of our books are kept "alive" and available unless and until an author requests a title be taken out of print.

We've learned a few things about independent publishing over the years. We've also evolved a unique and resilient publishing model that allows us to focus mainly on vetting and preserving for posterity poetry collections of exceptional quality without becoming overwhelmed with bookkeeping and mailing, fundraising activities, or taxing editorial and production "bubbles." To find out more, come see us at futurecycle.org.

www.ingramcontent.com/pod-product-compliance
Lightning Source LLC
Chambersburg PA
CBHW072141090426
42739CB00013B/3246